Gail Baker

Three Weavers

Three Weavers

Joan Potter Loveless

UNIVERSITY OF NEW MEXICO PRESS
ALBUQUERQUE

Library of Congress Cataloging-in-Publication Data

Loveless, Joan Potter, 1925–
Three weavers/Joan Potter Loveless.—1st ed.
    p.   cm.
Includes index.
ISBN 0–8263–1318–3
1. Hand-weaving—New Mexico—Taos Region.
2. Weavers—New Mexico—Taos Region—Biography.
3. Taos Region (N.M.)—Social life and customs.
I. Title.
TT848.L68   1992
746.1'4'092278953—dc20
[B]   91–26721

"On Weaving" from *Wisdom and the Senses: The Way of Creativity,*
Joan M. Erickson, © 1988 by Joan M. Erickson.
Reprinted by permission of W. W. Norton & Company.

Design by Susan Gutnik.

Contents

Color plates following page 110

To our children
Kimry, Jenny, Conor
Ian
Seth, Kinlock, Lorelei
and to our grandchildren
Rochelle, Teresa, Tyler

Joan Loveless with Navajo Country. *Photo by Mildred Tolbert.*
Courtesy of The Harwood Foundation, Taos, New Mexico.

Preface

M any people have in some way helped me in the writing of this book. First, of course, I want to thank the two weavers and good friends, Rachel Miller Brown and Kristina Brown Wilson for their help in remembering how things were. I would also like to thank Tricia Hurst for her early reading of the manuscript and George Zopf for patiently introducing me to, and often rescuing me from, my word processor.

Very special thanks go to Doone Williams, who has read and reread the manuscript, and whose perception and encouragement have been of enormous value.

My one regret is that this is of necessity an incomplete story, that I have not been able to tell of the work and the contributions of the many other weavers and spinners, past and present, who have been part of the story of weaving in New Mexico.

Most of all, I thank my husband, David, without whose help and support the writing of this book might not have happened at all.

◗ ◗ ◗

If we had lived in India, perhaps we would have become involved with cotton, if in China or Japan, with silk. It was important that our wool was the local, the native, thread—that it was grown here, that the sheep grazed on this land that was watered by the winter snows of these mountains beneath which we lived. The woolen thread that we came to love was a product of this culture, a part of its history, part of the breathing and the life of this valley. Weaving tapestries about what I saw here, it made sense to blend all of the elements from which the wool came back into images of what appeared to me to be going on in this valley and the land and sky that I could see from it. It was a combining of the messages from the land with the woolen fiber, translated through the colors that it could be given, into the arrangements of spaces and shapes that were suggested to me by what I saw as time passed here.

◗ ◗ ◗

Arrival

It may be that there is a place somewhere for everyone that feels like their proper location, their beginning. Taos Valley is mine. Here I feel that I am in my correct relation to the Other Than Me—surrounded by The Story, whatever the story is. I recognize that *my* mysteries reside here, that everything I don't understand is somehow going on here. This happens as time takes place with the traveling of the sun through the day, with the brilliance of the stars somewhere within the great space of night over this high land, with the transformations of rock and dirt and dust and air and living tree and dry wood and weed and bright green of spring—all of these breathing together, weaving back and forth through the year, woven by this space and this place into a great riddle that is beginning and ending and forever.

I first came to the Taos Valley almost forty years ago with my husband, the painter Oli Sihvonen, and our ten-month-old daughter, Kimry. We had heard of northern New Mexico as a place where the air was clear and bright and, on that recommendation, decided to go there from college for a year of getting our bearings before going on to more serious things. We made contact with a painter, Louis Ribak, who lived in Taos, a small town north of the capital of Santa Fe; so that became our destination. We had bought an old Model A convertible in New England and driven it back to school—Black Mountain College in North Carolina. It performed beautifully on that trip, so we decided to take it west.

Entering New Mexico from the south, through El Paso, Texas, was traveling gradually into a different world for us. We drove between dry, rocky, layered hills for a time, then through long, plain stretches where the small towns looked smaller and the roads between them became threads, like lines on a large diagram show-

1

ing the simplest connection between two points. Occasionally we drove alongside the Rio Grande, its waters hurrying past us toward the Gulf of Mexico, we hurrying toward its source in the high country to the north. Traveling became a continually unfolding inspection of the contours of the earth, and we began to relate to the far distance—the horizon—and with the space came a stillness. We had come a long way from the heavily wooded mountains of western North Carolina, damply craggy and filled with mirroring vistas. Under a clear sky we put the car top down, and it was warm in the September sun.

Until we passed Albuquerque we felt rather than saw the rise in altitude, but now we were clearly climbing, the road following and sometimes cutting through the tilting land as it became foothills to a rising range of mountains on the east. Features of the landscape altered in our view as we approached and then passed them; it seemed that there was no such thing as a constant point of view in this country. It seemed that only by staying absolutely still could one put a name or a definition to an image—and even then the passage of time and the events of weather would alter what one thought one had seen, as with the changing shadows on the forms of the land as the afternoon progressed.

In Santa Fe we seemed to have crossed a border into another time as well as place. Narrow streets ambled between adobe buildings, leading us to the main plaza, shady with trees, benches along the paths bisecting it from side to side and corner to corner. Along the streets facing the plaza were low, connected adobe buildings whose long portals, or porches, shaded the sidewalks. Peaks of the range of mountains we had been following rose to the east, their pinon-covered foothills flowing down into the earthen town. The air felt different; we were now at an altitude of 7,500 feet.

Our destination was still seventy miles to the north, and soon we were following the Rio Grande through small villages and valley farms. Dry hills rose on our right, a strange landscape that looked as though it had given up all of its form and fertility in the ancient past. The valley along the banks of the river widened and narrowed and widened again, then became a broad, fertile strip of orchard farms with a maze of small roads wandering between them past adobe houses and village clusters. Beyond this valley rose dry mesas and hills, and finally the Rio Grande disappeared behind one of these and we began to climb again, the road a continuous series of steep, blind curves.

Then suddenly we emerged from the canyon and pulled over to the side of the road to stare in amazement. Before us lay the most broadly beautiful place I had ever seen. Open, the land stretched off for perhaps a hundred miles to the north and west. On our right the ranges we had been following continued, then gave way to towering masses of peaks, the whole bending to form a crescent toward the west, enclosing a broad shallow valley in which the only hint of habitation was the dark strands that indicated trees fanning out from the foothills.

Circling the valley a great sagebrush plain flowed on and on to the far horizon, where it was rimmed by other mountain ranges so far away that they appeared to be featureless cutouts of pale blue silk. This desert floor, which at first seemed to be flat, gradually as we looked became a flowing surface of slightest undulations, cloud shadows moving over it like enormous birds; then finally we saw the canyon of the Rio Grande as an intermittent slash across it from north to south, sometimes invisible and then, with a jog that threw shadow on a cut edge, appearing again. Here and there rose single low mountains, flared out where their evergreens met the desert floor and rising to single peaks or knobs like long-extinct volcanoes, which we later learned they indeed were.

Over all the years since then, this first view of Taos Valley has lost none of its wonder. With every return the reaching of this plateau after climbing out of the canyon produces the same exhilaration, the same levitation of spirit. At that point I can comprehend a little the Indian origin stories of the People coming out of the earth to their home on the surface.

We realized that Taos must lie at the foot of the crescent of mountains, amongst the trees, but we were still too far away to be sure. We drove on, dipping once more into a canyon before the road finally became straight, heading across rolling sagebrush land until we reached the beginnings of an adobe village.

❿ ❿ ❿

Ranchos de Taos lay within and along the ridges above a long valley extending from the mountains, watered by a stream that came from them. There we found Louis Ribak, who had located a house for us nearby. We followed him along a road above the valley and pulled in beside a long, low adobe house nestled near the edge of the ridge, overlooking the long valley and the matching ridge on the other side—dotted also with low adobe houses, sometimes clinging to the slope itself. Ours was an old house, very little modernized—a series of single rooms across its width with deep windows and doorways through the thick earthen walls. Beyond the kitchen was another apartment, where the painter Leo Garel would soon come to live. Otherwise, our part of the house contained a small bedroom and a lovely long el-shaped room with an arched adobe fireplace built into a jog in the outer wall. The whole interior wall surface was plastered with a soft pearl-grayish-white earth, flecked with tiny bits of mica that caught the light. Each room had a small north window framing our view of the broad, more or less symmetrical Taos Mountain, the sacred mountain of the Taos Pueblo Indians, Louis told us. A larger window had been put into the west wall of the living room, and from it we could look past the houses along the ridge to the desert, which was to become our favorite view—the place of change and mystery.

Looking becomes an intermittently full-time occupation in this valley, and that was the day it began for us. At all times of the day, with any alteration in the weather, the scene was changed in some way, somewhere. It seemed that we had found a setting that would be forever a visual laboratory for us—one that could never be exhausted of its questions, its suggestions and illusions, its contrasts and mysteries. At some point Oli arrived at the most briefly apt description of it all—it was a place of *active serenity*.

We settled into our new home happily—our house of earth. The mica flickered dimly when we made a fire with the pinon wood Louis had brought us for the fireplace. Pinon burns very fragrantly; we were to become familiar with this scent over the valley on winter mornings and evenings.

We explored the neighborhood on foot, absorbing the unfamiliar sights. The settlements along the road were continuous from the town all the way to the foothills where the road climbed, finally, into the mountains. We learned that Ranchos de Taos (Ranches of Taos) was, according to Indian tradition, originally founded by members of Taos Pueblo to take advantage of the

good farming land in the valley, and we wondered if their ancestors had perhaps also farmed there in the distant past when a
pueblo stood above its southern ridge. Later, it became a Spanish
village, and there the mountain men came for supplies for their
season of beaver trapping in the surrounding mountains. In the
center of the town is the Saint Francis of Assisi Mission, built by
the Franciscans. Over the years it fell into disrepair, then was
rebuilt around 1772. It is an impressive structure—120 feet long,
with exceptionally thick walls supported by great abutments and
originally surrounded by a six-foot adobe wall. Now much pho-
tographed and painted, it is one of the most beautiful adobe buildings in northern New Mexico.

Most of the houses that dotted the ridge were simple, flat-
roofed adobe rectangles with rooflines indented here and there
with *canales* or channels in the firewall to carry off water and
rising sometimes at a corner to enclose a chimney. But adobe
lends itself to variation, and this basic rectangle had often been
extended, with the growth of families or with new owners, with
an added ell, as in our house, or another rectangle stepped slightly
down or up to accommodate itself to the lay of the land. Sometimes a whole series of additions blended one building into another—turning, changing levels, enclosing courtyards with high
arched gateways—all of adobe and all mudded over to make
smooth joinings of horizontals and verticals. Everywhere the
workings of the hands of man and woman were apparent in this
raising of structures out of the earth itself. Each building had a
particular character in its lines—here, more square, more precise—there, the curves more pronounced or more flowing.

Above us small dirt roads led through the intricacies of Rio
Chiquito. We followed them, walking the boundaries of people's
domains—beside the adobe wall of a house, along the low wall
of its courtyard and a gate, past a corral, where between the
vertical poles we could glimpse sheep or chickens and stacks of
hay. Each house was built according to its particular situation and
needs, and the road made its path around whatever angle the
house happened to occupy. The roads had simply grown from
foot and horse paths to cartways and now accommodated modern
cars if driven with an eye to dips, bends, and ruts. Sometimes
the road would follow an irrigation ditch for a while and then
make a sudden turn to cross it and climb, then bend again and

travel along a higher level. In this meandering manner access to all of the homes of a village was eventually accomplished, and we wandered over all the roads within a few miles of our house in all directions, finding the crossings that made it possible to make larger or smaller loops out and back. There were days when a walk down the dry, gravelly ridge below us leading to the long quiet lanes between fields in the valley seemed the thing to do. On others, perhaps in the late afternoon, we would walk up to the top of Rio Chiquito, finally coming out into the sagebrush and wandering far enough into it to watch the wildly colorful sunset out over the desert on our way back.

Kimry enjoyed most of these walks from Oli's shoulders, from where she greeted everyone along the road. We learned, though, that in these intimate byways that often passed close by open doors and windows, walkers nodded minimally to those they met, not interrupting their privacy. The older people, especially, seemed to walk a lot—not in a hurry, but walking as though there was a point to that in itself. They, particularly, responded to Kimry's greetings, so she became our emissary and soon we had many nodding acquaintances. Intermittently, from early morning until dark people walked, or rather strolled, past the various houses we were to live in over the years across the larger valley.

Beyond Taos Mountain rose other peaks—a curving saddle above the treeline, an isolated tooth of rock—then after a canyon deep into the mass of the range, the last formation within our view stretched, its foothills descending in a silhouette pointing toward the desert and the pinon-covered triangles that made up its form rising one behind and above another to finally be crowned by Lobo Peak. We saw on those upper slopes great swaths of what appeared to be fields of golden flowers, then learned that they were the twinkling autumn gold leaves of groves of aspen trees. This was the panorama to which we looked between the activities of our days—this series of surging forms, so solid but so ephemeral with the changes in their appearance. The peaks drew the weather to them and around them it dispersed; the heights received the first snow, and always they caught the first rays of morning light as the sun climbed in the east and the last glow of the day after the valley where we lived was already shaded by the western horizon. So the mountains added a bit of glory to our mornings and evenings, showing us the up-slanting light of early morning and the last flares in the evening as the sun seemed to boil away beyond the thin line of mountains far in the west.

The vast expanse of the desert was another source of wonder that we became acquainted with in those first weeks. In a way it told best of all the story of the mystery in which we lived. It seemed to tell it more through space than form, though of course it was that also—form stretched out so far that it seemed to include time within its space. On it the dramas of light and weather were played, seemingly without limits. Storms with towering dark clouds dropping gray curtains of rain, or whiter ones of snow, would be isolated and then move, slowly traveling for perhaps fifty miles before changing shape or clearing. As we watched the changes over its breadth we became acquainted with illusion, with transformation, with vacancy, with large serenity, with some faint comprehension of reality as an unending interplay of forces and elements that allowed us to experience beauty and wonder and to feel ourselves part of the mystery that we witnessed.

Winter

We settled down for the winter in our warm little house, got in a supply of pinon wood and relished its smell in our fireplace, explored the town of Taos and the network of other villages on dirt roads that laced the length of the valley.

Streams flowed out of the creases between the major masses of the mountains and fanned out to the west and south, etching their ways along the paths of least resistance, finally dropping miles later down through side canyons in narrow, grassy beds to join the Rio Grande at the bottom of the great gorge. These streams—Rio Hondo, Arroyo Seco, Rio Pueblo, Rio Fernando, Rio Grande del Rancho—had determined the settlement of the valley. Along them, beginning with the Indian Pueblo, the original town, houses were dotted next to fields that were irrigated from their waters, and here and there along the way tiny villages happened. So the courses of the streams were also, more or less, the courses of the roads, with a few added to connect the fanning web of streams. From higher vantage points this total pattern could be read by the lines of cottonwoods that thrived along the streams. We wandered these byways happily, fascinated with all that was different: the village clusters with their tiny lanes curling between brown or tan adobe houses, each shaped to accommodate to its particular setting, but all blending in their common material.

It was like living in a foreign country in many ways, and we enjoyed the anonymity of being part of the minority element in this setting. Spanish, which we didn't speak, was the primary local language still; the Indians spoke it as well as their own language, Tiwa. The affairs of Taos town, the commercial center, had been, I suppose, for many years carried on in both Spanish and English, but our little village area of Talpa was still primarily Spanish-speaking at home. Kimry worked out communication with our neighbors and their children. She was something of a curiosity with her blondness, and through her we also advanced to friendly greetings from dooryard to dooryard.

Gradually we became acquainted with other outsiders who had made the valley their home. Leo Garel arrived to live in the other apartment of our house, and with him we began a friendship that was to continue for many years and in other places. Just below us, in a large rambling adobe clinging to the brink of the ridge, lived Barbara and Howard Cook, both painters. They had added onto their original small house over the years—a studio above, another below, little patios where a nook was formed by the shape of the house. Lovely old weavings and other artifacts of the area hung on the walls and lay on the polished adobe floors or occupied small niches hollowed out of the walls.

One day Howard invited us to go with him to visit some friends and pick apples on their ranch at the other end of the valley, on the foothills below Lobo Peak. North of Taos we left the highway on a dirt road that climbed amongst the pinons up a finger of the rise between arroyos and came into the open again into fields surrounding a large, two-story, pitched-roof adobe farmhouse, then into the woods again for another climb to the ranch itself. It was a breath-taking spot. A small adobe and log ranch house sat, barn and sheds behind it, looking over an orchard and cleared land to an incredibly vast western view across the desert to the far mountains. Pinon woods enclosed it on each side, with some cleared fields, and behind it the mountain rose, with rock cliffs and tall ponderosa pines.

Rachel and Bill Hawk, surprisingly pink-skinned and Bill with slightly graying hair, smiling and friendly in a reticent way, both seemed to carry the imprint of this remote place with its high, fresh air and its extraordinary view of the world below.

Bill was born and had grown up in the farmhouse we had passed, then with Rachel had built this cabin where they raised their two children. Now they lived alone and ran the place by themselves, happily isolated by heavy snows for many weeks through the winters, and in any season leaving their mountain only for buying necessities and an occasional visit in the valley. They gave the impression that they had been created by this situation—this scene, this air, their active life and their small house, neat and cozy. I wasn't surprised, though, to learn that Rachel came from New England; there was a touch of that, also, about the place. We had cake and coffee, then picked apples from the orchard below the house—an adventure for Kimry, who had not until then really understood that apples grew on trees and then fell, to be hidden in the curling leaves and deep orchard grass.

Howard wanted to pick up a pack that he had left in a cabin the Hawks owned a little farther up the mountain, so Bill drove up with us. The road climbed beside a thin stream and emerged in a clearing of mixed trees, grass, and sagebrush, just beside the cabin. It stood like an ark beached on Mount Ararat, a two-story box built of logs, each wall with a bank of windows in its center, a barely slanting roof looking as though it was attached only temporarily atop the box, and a small porch along the side, sheltering the door. A wire fence separated the sagebrush and chamisa growing within the yard from that which grew outside it. "To keep out the cows," Bill explained.

Over the gateway was nailed a faded sign that read, "The Tower Beyond Tragedy." Inside, the downstairs was divided by a partial wall to separate the kitchen, with a large black iron cookstove, from the sitting room, furnished with a table and some chairs and the grandest view of the land to the west that I had yet seen. Tiny stairs led to the top floor and a screen-walled room or sleeping porch containing only a bed and a rocking chair and what was surely the most superb view a house was ever built to accomplish—almost 360 degrees, all the way around to the backdrop of mountains behind Taos, soaring across the desert to the Jemez Mountains, pale in the distance, and farther to the north past the foothills. It really seemed like heaven. Behind the porch was another room, looking up the mountain, again more windows than walls, and flooded with light.

Howard gathered his belongings, and Oli waited until we were back in the car to ask, as though it was a casual afterthought, if it might be possible to rent the cabin sometime. We held our breath as Bill answered, "Maybe. Call us in the spring to see if our daughter wants it."

On the way back to Taos Howard told us the story of the cabin. A young English painter, Dorothy Brett, had come to Taos years ago with D. H. and Frieda Lawrence, who came at the urging of Mabel Dodge Luhan. A patroness of the arts and collector of people, Luhan had made Taos her home, marrying a

Taos Indian, Tony Luhan. The Lawrences had spent some of their stay in New Mexico at the ranch adjoining the Hawks's belonging to Mabel, and Brett, as she was called, often stayed there with them. These three women—Mabel, Frieda, and Brett—carried on over the years a vigorous and sometimes bitter rivalry for first place in Lawrence's creative configuration, a rivalry that continued even after his death, when Frieda returned to Taos to live. The story went that at some point Frieda turned Brett out of the establishment at Mabel's ranch, and the Hawks, then a young couple, let her build a cabin for herself on their land.

Brett stayed on in Taos and we later knew her, enjoyed her, and respected her work tremendously. She was one of the more or less realistic painters who really achieved the quality of light, space, and color of the Southwest in her canvases. She made wonderful paintings of the Indian dances—bright, simple, and powerful. It seemed that she was able to paint the Indian ceremonies in a way that did not attempt to portray their *intent* from inside, but rather to convey her sense of them within their environment, their space, an approach that was very successful. She loved color and used it well. Taos became her home and she stayed for the rest of her life.

When we got back to Talpa, Howard helped us to pick out the rocky cliffs on the mountainside just above the cabin and the tin roof of the big farmhouse below the ranch, which caught the setting sun. He told us that when snow fell we would see the fields beside it as a white patch in the midst of the pinon woods. We wrapped our supply of apples in newspaper and stored most of them away in the undergrund pumphouse just outside our kitchen door.

Our Model A proved to be a perfect vehicle for exploring the new terrain. It had a high axle and could navigate almost any kind of road, from the rocky tracks in the mountains to the deepest mire that any of the dirt roads might turn to during thaws. Its greatest virtue, though, was that with the top down we were very little separated from whatever we were exploring.

We drove into the mountain canyons and over the mountains to see the villages on the other side—Penasco, Las Trampas, and Truchas. Beyond the valley, we followed little dirt tracks up onto the mesa, the beginning of the sagebrush country in the distance that we called The Desert. Two roads, one in the north and the other to the south of Ranchos de Taos, led out to the rim of the Rio Grande Gorge, then tortuously descended the wall of the canyon in a series of acute hairpin turns to reach the river, crossed over on bridges, and as tortuously ascended the other side. Once, halfway down, we passed a school bus backing up carefully to align itself for navigating one of the curves and wondered how it managed in the winter snow. On the other side there were many tracks to follow, often those of sheep herders who camped out with their flocks in this seeming wasteland. In this way we ranged over all the land within sight of our home in the valley, a little surprised that this closer acquaintance in no way diminished its mysteries and the charm of its illusions.

Finally the snows came. Clouds gathered over the mountains—over the Truchas far to the south, over the Jemez on the western horizon, over *our* mountains. There was talk of snow and we watched the clouds and felt a kind of levitation in the air. Those to the south began to take on a new kind of shape, their edges smooth and drawn out as though they were being sculpted by the air around them. Later, we became used to these clouds presaging snow and called them Brancusi clouds. They had the feel of Brancusi sculptures, long and elegantly shaped and full of smooth tension where their edges met the surrounding air.

Gradually the clouds multiplied and diffused to become total environment and then finally, magically, flakes of white began to fall, bringing an early dusk. All the details of our usual world were gone—no mountain, no desert—just the immense minutiae of these silent bits of white falling onto the brown earth, against brown adobe walls, through leafless trees. Quiet, utter quiet. There was no wind, just this silent falling, coming with the night, its silence making almost a sound of listening. All night long snow fell through the darkness.

In the morning light poured in; the snowing was over. Remnants of cloud still hung beyond the desert; there were long rolls of vapor clinging to the tops of our mountains. Above the treeline the peaks were crystalline white, and with no wind yet risen, even the evergreen-covered slopes were heavy with white. Our world had returned, transformed. Around us every surface was piled high with pure white. Every adobe edge was thickly and precisely outlined; snow lay deep beside every adobe wall. In the valley below, a white lace that was the hedgerows drew out the shapes of the fields—pure white rectangles, sometimes with clusters of house, shed, and corral tucked into their corners. That early morning the only earth to be seen was what had been raised up to house man or beast. All of the wide Taos Valley was carpeted and from each village rose trails of pinon smoke as the day began, fragrant in the winter air.

The main roads were soon plowed and movement about the valley resumed. But that year, the small roads and pathways where we took our walks stayed a hard-packed white for most of the winter. Temperatures were low and walks shorter, but the lanes and byways, the houses and walls, the ditches and hedgerows, were over and over again set off by fresh snowfalls, delightful in the midday sun. The simplest visual memory of that winter became that of a band of golden earth wall topped precisely with a band of new brilliant snow, meeting the bluest of skies.

Time for Work

O li set up a studio space in the corner of our long room by the window facing the grand desert view and began making studies for paintings.

Though I didn't work with wool at all that year, the tapestries that I would later weave in the valley were already beginning to form. I think that I worked on them with my eyes as I watched what happened in this new world that we had found. The wool on the backs of the sheep that I saw every day would one day turn out to be my natural working material, but I didn't know that yet.

I had studied weaving with Anni Albers at Black Mountain College and had also taken Josef Albers's color, design, and drawing classes, all of which were very important for my later work. I loved the weaving process in general, but from the very beginning I somehow knew that what I really wanted eventually to do was to weave tapestries. It was to be a long time before I would own a loom on which to do this, and in the intervening years I simply worked with threads of one sort or another, finding or inventing various kinds of frames or structures on which to construct some form of textile.

Anni's weaving course began with focusing on two of the basic elements of weaving—texture and construction. We started by making texture studies, using all sorts of materials—from paper, on which we created texture by pricking with a pin, to seeds and grains, sand, bits of bark—anything that could be glued down to create variations of texture and tune us in to this quality that was important in weaving. Then we began to study weaving theory, on paper, becoming familiar with the construction of the traditional weaves, and at the same time started working on looms with the wide variety of yarns that filled the shelves down one side of the large weaving room. When the warp on our loom was used up, we learned to put on a warp with the help of Anni or some experienced student. In our theory classes we sometimes, as a group, designed weavings for some particular textile need, such as a theatre curtain, figuring out how to achieve the necessary qualities of design, wearability, and sound absorption.

There are many good ways of teaching weaving, whether as a basic general introduction to the discipline, for a particular type of weaving career such as designing for industry, or for the mastering of some specific technique of the craft of weaving. For me the method Anni used was a very congenial one, a broad introduction to the possibilities inherent in the medium that generated ideas for going ahead with directions that particularly fascinated me, aided by the wonderful teaching of Josef Albers in "learning to see," in the development of visual curiosity.

Someone once brought me, from some tropical place, a curious piece of fibrous husk from a coconut palm. It was composed of two sets of fibers that lay at right angles across each other, naturally annealed together and, though dry, still somewhat pliable so that the squares formed by the crossing fibers could be flexed to become diamonds, much as screening or gauze cloth can be stretched "out of shape." This reminded me of the first definition of weaving that I was given as a student: "Weaving is the interpenetration of two sets of threads at right angles to each other." The difference is that these fibers, rather than interlocking, simply lay upon each other and were held together by some sort of plant juices. Where these coconut palms grow, the fibers of both the leaf and the husk are used for weaving hats and mats. I have always imagined that such patterns of growth in plants and the materials of which they are composed were observed and employed in the beginnings of weaving.

What we call weaving is, in its simplest terms, this arrangement of one set of threads—the *warp*—wound between two sticks or the opposite sides of a frame, so that another thread—the *weft*—can be woven over and under, alternate threads of the warp to form a piece of fabric—small or large, fine or coarse, depending on the fiber used and the purpose for which it is needed. On this simple principle of "over and under" is based the whole history of textile making, varying in both time and place as to its appearance, its cultural significance, and its level of development.

The terms used in the craft of weaving and the related textile arts—heddles and treadles and shuttles and such—are names for the tools that have been invented to keep the threads or fibers in order and to lead them in the paths that they must take to become textiles.

By means of these tools a vast range of fabrics or textiles can be made: the gossamer web of a silken sari, the deep rich pile of an oriental carpet, the coarse rough plain weave of a grain sack. And the looms on which these things are created vary enormously from the earliest known type—the vertical warp-weighted loom, in which the warp threads were secured only to a top beam and hung from there with their ends weighted in groups. There are Greek vase paintings from the fifth century B.C. showing these in use, and the remains of such looms have also been found in the sites of ancient Swiss lake villages, as well as in the Near East, North Africa, and the Americas. Somewhere between this simple early loom and modern mechanized weaving machines, made entirely of metal and merely attended by a human being, lies the domain of the contemporary handweaver, the person who enjoys working with fibers or threads and exploring the making of them into objects of use and enjoyment.

The looms devised by nomads are vastly different from the looms of the Renaissance on which tapestries were woven. The nomadic weavers needed to be able to dismantle their weaving structure and roll it up so that it could be moved without messing up the threads of a partly woven piece; the tapestry weaver's loom stayed in place and could have a wide warp of fine threads, wide enough for a row of women to work, side by side, creating a complex woven picture that would, when done, cover a whole wall.

Weaving has, through history as well as now, been done by both women and men, although in some cultures it is done predominantly by one or the other. The fibers used traditionally within a culture or an area, of course, have depended on geographic conditions—where cotton or flax grew, where sheep were native, where silkworn culture developed. As "civilization" spread, methods and materials were traded and mixed, and adjustments of old techniques to the addition of new ones through the centuries slowly altered the distinctly native textile practices, both enriching and diluting them.

Of course, through the long history and prehistory of the textile arts there were variations of textile construction that employed, not sets of interpenetrated threads at right angles to each other, but various kinds of twining and knotting into the warp strung onto the loom. And before the invention of the loom the ancient ancestors of every culture worked with some kind of finger-woven netting—braiding, plaiting, and interweaving—using whatever fibers were available in the flora and fauna of their region. From these materials they devised ways to construct things they needed—twine and rope, nets and bags, sandals and baskets.

Even though, in one sense, the "evolution" of handweaving can be seen as a progression toward more ease, more efficiency, with the development of equipment and tools that accomplish these things, this is not a true picture of what weaving is all about. Weaving in the present is also, and most importantly, all of the minute, separate, weaving occurrences that have gone on in the past, all of the particular, individual, bits and pieces that have been woven in the past by people sitting at looms or simply twining fibers into some form. The satisfaction that we derive from being involved in a piece of weaving is exactly the same satisfaction that weavers always have derived from their work. Our work is no better; often it is not nearly as good. Weaving is not involved with the concept of progress; it is much more concerned with holding still the moment, with savoring and with marking it, with this still very simple participation with the fibers that we find around us.

That first year in Taos I, too, needed such a simple participation for the pieces of time that were available between other activities. I wanted to get to work in this earthen house that had become such a home as winter enclosed it. I had a small hand-smoothed walnut table loom that Oli's sister, Mim Sihvonen, had made for me in the wood shop at Black Mountain College. On it I wove cloth for bags and pillows and a bit of blue and green checked woolen for backs to deerskin mittens that we made for Kimry.

Then at El Mercado, the ten-cent store on the plaza in Taos, I discovered the perfect material for my winter's work—cotton carpet warp in a surprisingly wide range of soft, clear colors. I wanted to explore something, not just weave more small pieces of cloth, so I would try using the carpet warp with some card weaving cards that I had acquired somewhere but never used.

Card weaving is an ancient technique. It is thought that it was invented by the Egyptians; traces of its use have been found in their tombs from 4000 B.C. The American Indians used the method, making the cards of square, flat pieces of shell, drilling a hole in each corner; my modern ones were made of cardboard. This technique produces a band or strap that is very strong, and colors can be threaded through the cards so as to form patterns. When the cards stand side by side, the lined-up holes carry the threads and do the work, which on a regular floor loom is done by a complex array of heddles, frames, and treadles. I couldn't have found a simpler weaving machine.

I picked a few colors for stripes and measured out the required threads, strung them through the cards in the prescribed order and when the hanks were combed smooth, tied each end to a large hook fastened to a door frame, pulled up a chair, and was ready to weave.

Ancient weaving techniques are not necessarily simple ones, in fact often quite the contrary is so—witness the complex textiles of South America, the Incas in particular, some of them still unsolved textile puzzles. But this technique was not one of those designed for exquisite complexity. It had been arrived at in various cultures as the simplest and best way to produce a certain kind of result—an extremely strong strap, band, or belt. It was portable, could be set up anyplace where there were two stable spots to tie it onto, and one of those could be the weaver's own body. For more complex weaving I would have needed a more complex machine, but I specifically wanted just to explore in the simplest way possible. Simplicity at this point was for me not abbreviation but a way to really focus on something in order to learn about it, to study this one specific kind of textile and to become acquainted with it and what could be done with it. It was a supreme, luxurious, indulgence.

For several months I worked just with stripes; each band that I wove suggested something new to try, and I wound colored threads around a piece of cardboard to plan widths and colors that seemed intriguing. I discovered that I could create new colors by mixing; by alternating single lines of two colors, say a pink and an orange, across the band I could create a soft coral-colored belt. This was such a nice combination that I wove Kimry a pair of suspenders with it.

These bands were woven color studies, really—continuations of work done in Josef Albers's color class. Those classes were wonderful. We collected colored papers and used them to study how color behaved. We learned how colors changed when the color next to them changed, how different colors could appear to become the same when influenced by neighboring colors, how intensity or quiet was built up, how the appearance of depth happened as we cut papers into shapes and strips, bringing in the influence of size and form. We played with stripes, learning to cause them to appear to be a smooth and level surface or to undulate or step with changes in widths or adjoining colors. Albers was both a disciplined and a passionate teacher, and his excitement with color, and the learning that it produced, was very infectious. Often he would jump up from his chair with delight when a student produced some unexpected result, exclaiming, "See! Look what that little color has done! It doesn't have to be bright to be powerful. Just like people!"

I was practicing now for working with color in tapestries later, storing up experience and familiarity. As I worked, I also saw these color phenomena happening in the world around me, and this small, focused work was a wonderful contrast to the other absorption of that year—watching what went on in the large and open world of this valley that we had come to. It seemed to me that it was like playing scales must be for a musician, tuning one in to slight variations, to the influences of notes on each other in different sequences and intervals. Years later, this way of achieving just the effect I needed in a color's edge or between two areas of color would be very valuable to me, an integral part of my way of working.

The strips usually became belts, just tied at first and then we thought we might be able to sell some of the surplus, so Oli made leather tabs for them with holes for thong laces. We sold some in stores in Taos, a welcome addition to our slim budget. We got reorders and, to be more practical, I found some slightly heavier yarn, a soft natural jute, in a hardware store and began weaving with that. Down the road from us was a general store, Vigil's, and in an intricate old wooden case Mr. Vigil carried a vast spectrum of Putnam dyes. I started dyeing the jute in the colors I wanted and another dimension of working opened up.

During the winter we became good friends with Dixie and John Yaple, who lived not far from us, and we spent many evenings with them, engrossed in conversations around the fireplace, walking home by snowlight with Kimry bundled asleep in a blanket. John had somehow happened into Taos years before as a young man, loved it, and made it his home. He knew the surrounding country well, both mountains and prairie, as well as the Indian, Spanish, and Anglo old-timers who made up its culture, and he told us wonderful stories through those winter evenings.

Their house was a fine old adobe, and it was there that I first became acquainted with traditional Indian and Spanish weavings. There were fireplaces in every room, and the rooms were decorated with their wonderful collection of southwestern artifacts and with mineral specimens and other natural curiosities gathered on John's wanderings over the countryside. They also had a good library that they shared with us.

Dixie worked as personal secretary for Millicent Rogers, the Standard Oil heiress, who was building a house in Taos, dividing her time between there and New York. Millicent was also a collector of native southwestern work on a rather grand scale, and her collection years later would be housed in the museum bearing her name in Taos. But at that point she was a woman of wealth and fashion (at some point one of America's Best Dressed Women) who had been smitten with the area and spent part of her time in this out-of-the-way place. Dixie had seen the belts I was making and showed them to Millicent, who bought several and ordered more.

Then one day Dixie dropped by with a proposal for an interesting commission. It seemed that Millicent made as well as collected jewelry. She was preparing for a show of her work at Durlacher's in New York and for some heavy gold breastplates wanted something other than metal chains to hang them by. She designed elaborate pieces in silver and gold, had them made up in New York, and then worked them further herself, pounding in texture and adding detail.

"Could you, out of your rough yarn, make something ropey, like brazil nuts strung together?" Dixie asked. "Certainly," I said, and set about figuring out how. I gathered what textured string and yarn I could find locally and set to work, playing with knots and wrapping, happily exploring again—this time with textures and loom-less construction. Finally I came up with a strong, fairly stiff construction of jute with big, smooth knots separated by sections where the hank of threads was neatly bound around by a single thread. It was dramatic if a bit rugged and proved to be just what Millicent wanted, so I made up variations of it for several other pieces. For me it was a very happy cooperation. Nothing I could come up with was too outlandish for her, and I loved exploring what could be done with a set of materials. She had a wonderful sense for combining textures—fiber and metal and stone—and was great fun to work with, plucking ideas from one piece to try in another. Kimry found her fascinating and loved to go to her house where, among other delightful things, she experienced her first full-length mirror.

Millicent's most exciting and challenging request was an eight-inch-wide belt woven of heavy cording from the hardware store. It was a soft gray-tan color, designed for some specific use around the barn or corral that I have long forgotten. The belt was to be flared over the hips so that it could be worn low at the waist. She made a plate of pounded silver with two rows of mushroom-shaped knobs, to which I was to join the woven part of the belt with some kind of loops. It was quite an engineering feat to construct the flared sections with my weaving cards, but I finally managed it; then when the weaving was done I bound the threads into groups that ended with loops to fasten over the knobs. It was indeed a grand-looking object—resembling, perhaps, an ancient ceremonial belt, looking more like it had been dug up from an archaeological site than just made for a New York jewelry show.

Throughout the spring I worked at these fascinating commissions and also made more conventional belts for her. Often she wanted a particular belt in several sizes, for her ordinary clothes and for the full fiesta skirts that she usually wore when in Taos. By spring I was ready to retire my cards for a while.

In April, when green was beginning to slip across Taos Valley, the little field below the Hawk ranch appeared to have permanently turned from white to brown; we called the Hawks and learned that their daughter had other plans for the summer, so we could have the cabin. Rachel said we should give the road another two weeks to dry out, and then we could come up any time. Every day more green appeared in the valley below us, softening the landscape. The streams from the mountains flowed full and fast now as the snow above started to melt; a winter of heavy snows meant a summer of abundant water, and it had been a good winter.

Early in the spring men gathered to clear the irrigation ditches of the dry remains of last year's growth, freeing them of obstructions for the carrying of this new water, which as they worked was melting from the edges of the snow pack above them and bounding down the rocky stream beds toward the valley. The mountains not only lifted the spirit but fed the land as well. The streams fed the irrigation system, branching out at every stage of their descent from the foothills to water the fields of that level. The main artery was called the *Acequia Madre* or Mother Ditch, and from it water was let into smaller ditches by lifting a wooden ditch-gate and diverting the water. This apportioning of water was arranged within each small community, and was a matter of utmost importance. When the turn came to receive the water the farmer worked all the time it was flowing, moving over the land and directing the water over the area by creating small dikes with a shovel to soak it all before the ditch was turned off. The mountains provided grass for the sheep as well as water for the valley land. After the lambs were born and the shearing done, the flocks were taken up to the high meadows to graze for the summer.

Our first winter of work in Taos was over. The days were long and warm now, and we moved a table outside where we could watch the long shadows of the greening trees and hedgerows of the valley below and hear the sounds of evening as we ate our supper. In a few weeks we would move to the ranch for a leisurely summer of looking at the vast view, then move east again to rejoin the mainstream in the outer world and face the reality of making a living.

TOP: *Taos Mountain in winter.*
BOTTOM: *Ranchos de Taos valley, looking north over the Talpa ridge.*
Photos by Mildred Tolbert. Courtesy of The Harwood Foundation, Taos, New Mexico.

LEFT: *On the way to summer pasture in the mountains.*
BOTTOM: *Valdez Valley. The valley farms are watered by the Rio Hondo, emerging from the mountain canyon, upper right.*
Photos by Mildred Tolbert. Courtesy of The Harwood Foundation, Taos, New Mexico.

LEFT: *Joan in the Talpa house, winter of 1948.*
BOTTOM: *Joan card-weaving a belt.*

In Taos Again

I t was eight years later, in 1956, when we returned to Taos, again with a nine-month-old child, our second daughter, Jenny. Kimry was now eight. When we emerged from the canyon again, to see the valley spread out before us, it was a homecoming—a return to this beautiful place that had remained vividly alive for me over those years and to which I had always known I would have to return.

This time we lived in the village of Taos, in a small house of the Helene Wurlitzer Foundation, where Oli had a grant to paint for a year. Except for the less pastoral setting of our house, things seemed much the same—unpaved streets in most of the town, adobe houses, Taos Mountain looming above us, much nearer now. There were also more people our age now, young artists who had come here to concentrate on their work, accepting the difficulties of living on very little money as a reasonable exchange—even a welcome one—for a simple life rich in time. We looked up old friends and made new ones; Oli began showing his paintings in the Taos Art Association Gallery, and there soon would be several new galleries devoted exclusively to modern work.

Taos still felt much like a foreign country. The landscape, the architecture, the trilingual culture, and the blending of past and present provided by the presence of Spanish and Indian traditions all contributed to a feeling of separateness from the rest of the country. Northern New Mexico was far from airports and major highways and a certain insulation happened during the long drive north from Albuquerque and the rise in altitude as one approached this high land.

One of our friends from before was Lesley Brown, a painter. She was eager to take us out to Arroyo Seco to meet her son,

Malcolm, and his family, who had moved up from Albuquerque at the beginning of the summer and were building themselves a house, and her daughter, Kristina—a weaver—who lived near them. So one afternoon we drove north with her and turned off just before the village of Arroyo Seco and drove up a rocky, rutty road through a sub-village that Lesley told us bore two names, Dogtown and Lyman City. We then followed a lane between fields and stopped at a bushy hedge of willow and wild rose, almost hiding a ditch and the little footbridge that crossed it.

The house was large and dramatic, the walls still unplastered adobe brick. Lesley had told us that Malcolm and his wife, Rachel, had done all the building themselves. We liked them both immediately and they proudly showed us the house. It was one great round room, or rather it appeared so; actually it was a slight oval. The roof was supported by a huge central wood trunk on which rested large beams radiating to the outer walls. From beam to beam, the ceiling was formed of peeled aspen saplings, or *latillas*. One large slanting window was set over a platform on a giant windowsill that would become a bed, and through another light poured into what would be the kitchen. Opposite, was a *banco* or built-in adobe sofa, which would be cushioned and piled with pillows. It sat beside a large adobe fireplace that seemed to flow out of the wall.

An arched doorway that would eventually lead into another wing of the house now led to the family's living space—a large tent—and parked cozily next to that was a car with the seats removed, which had been made into, literally, a bed-room. The floor of the house was still loose dirt, and as someone had spilt a can of pepper there was a good deal of sneezing as we got acquainted. Their three children fitted in age just between our two—Jenny just a little younger than Lorelei, Kimry a year older than Seth, with Kinlock in the middle. For all of us, children as well as adults, it was the beginning of lifelong friendship.

It wasn't until another day that we met Kristina—tall, very blond and smiling, and very pregnant—and saw her little house. It was minimal, just a small rectangle that she and her husband, Bucky Wilson, had put up on an adjoining piece of land given to them by Malcolm and Rachel as a wedding present. Recently divorced, shy, and decidedly lonely as she waited for her child to be born, she welcomed new friends. For her, our arrival was very well-timed. Much later she described that to me as the most depressing time of her life.

> *I was living in one room with that loom—no lights, no electricity, not really a road, even. I'd work half the night because I couldn't sleep; I was desperately lonesome and that loom saved my life. Then you guys showed up. I distinctly remember the day you drove up in your old station wagon— when the drive used to go right behind my house. I saw this whole car full of blond, healthy-looking people, and thought—God, they look great.*

The house sat in a meadow, not far from the irrigation ditch that wound its way along the borders of meadows and fields, often as a hidden trickling stream beneath hedges of wild rose and willow arching from either side to form a shady channel. The section of ditch between Kristina and the Browns would become a favorite summer place for all of our children.

This meadowland, a sort of protected interior surrounded by the main roads to Arroyo Seco, to Valdez, and on up into the mountains and occasionally cut across by minor dirt roads or lanes, always seemed somehow charmed to me. There was a circularity to that land; it was centered on itself rather than being on the edge of something—a mountain, a stream, a ridge. The mountains, the desert, the far horizon—all of these were visible from within the meadow, but the nature of the meadow itself somehow slightly insulated it from the farther, dramatic views— tamed them somewhat. In the summertime this was particularly apparent when breezes tossed the meadow weeds in bloom, and the humming of insects cast a kind of spell. One day it occurred to me that the sights and sounds of a meadow must be much more dramatic and potent to a child, simply because his hands are down where he can stir the weeds and grasses when walking through them, and his eyes and nose are near enough to see and smell and get to know things.

We saw a lot of Kristina that winter; usually she would drop in when she came to town on an errand, and very soon it seemed that we had always been good friends. With the approach of the holidays we invented a wonderful money-making project. Oli and Kristina went up into the foothills and gathered all the va- rieties of evergreens they could find—mostly pinon and juniper—

and we spread them out over the floor of our living room and constructed fine, abundant, aromatic wreaths. When a batch of them was done, Kristina and Oli would gather them up over both arms and trudge off through the snow, selling them to the businesses and householders around the town. Kristina being seven months pregnant seemed to present a certain Mary and Joseph image, and they sold quite easily. The girls loved the fragrant disorder of an evergreen carpet, and when we had exhausted the market and netted a handsome seventy dollars apiece we tacked the remains up around the house and completed our other Christmas preparations.

That was the year that I began another aromatic Christmas tradition—the making of *pulla,* or Finnish coffee bread. Oli's sister, Mim, finally talked their Finnish mother into committing her recipe into a written scheme of measurements and sent me a copy. Pulla is a braided yeast loaf, flavored with freshly ground cardamom and sprinkled with chopped almonds and sugar, a wonderful delicate flavor. Finns use it as a daily bread, with coffee; in fact, coffee is seldom drunk without a slice of pulla in hand. Each fresh batch of loaves is critically examined by the baker when it comes out of the oven, its variation from the ideal observed, and then it is enjoyed with coffee. When it has lost some of its freshness, the remaining loaves are sliced and slowly toasted in the oven, thereby producing *korpulla,* which is eaten until the next batch of pulla is baked. Korpulla is most often dunked in coffee, and I discovered it makes a fine teething bread, like melba toast. In our family pulla became one of the basic requirements for the creation of Christmas. At that time cardamom was not readily available as a spice as it is now, and Mim suggested trying a pharmacy for it as it is used to flavor medicines, and that was where we found it. So that Christmas the smell of baking pulla was added to the scents of greens and the wintersmell of pinon fires.

This was before the time of wood stoves coming back into use, and the smell of woodsmoke that we enjoyed was mostly from adobe fireplaces. Most of the houses had fireplaces, adobe ones usually built into a corner of the room, blending into a wall of the same material—a simple rounded arch over the firebox, a low rounded hearth—these elements showing the mark of some individual maker, giving each fireplace its own personality. Sometimes seats of adobe were built along the wall on either side, making the coziest of sitting corners on blustery winter nights. Another variation was the built-in sofa or *banco,* such as the Browns were building, constructed of adobe and finished with cushions and pillows.

The adobe walls both looked and felt warm, and the traditional houses were cozy in the winter with stored heat as well as cool in the summer. There is a special quality to adobe walls, a kind of liveness, that comes from both the material itself and the form-ing of them by hand-smoothing of the plaster layer over the earth bricks. They are smooth but not rigid; the corner line where wall meets wall is a clean line that again benefits from being formed by hand. There is a subtle *path* to it, slight but still there. After the plastering coat goes on the walls, a coat of earth paint makes the final surface. *Tierra blanca* covered the inside walls of our first house in Talpa, over the Ranchos de Taos valley. Though it is called white, it is actually more of a silvery mercurial color, fine and flecked with bits of mica. With every changing light of the day and every bend of the walls, it varies from its whitest color to faint grays and shadows. After living within these walls for many years, rooms made with walls of precise sheet materials come to seem like arbitrary divisions of some larger space rather than natural enclosures, each with its own center.

I was still a loomless weaver and, as usual, found things to make with threads in my spare time. We needed lampshades, and I concocted some out of leftover jute and linen yarn from belt making. I had played around with knotting in various ways and had come up with interesting results, which I later saw as the new rage called macrame. I had happened onto working with knots when tying a package for the mail; there was extra string after I tied the knot, and I had simply kept knotting and gotten fascinated with the variations I came up with and then made a frame on which to work on squares or rectangles. So to concoct a lampshade now, I tried knotting into yarn wound around an old lampshade frame. It worked well, diffusing light pleasantly, the knots making a spiraling line of pattern. I am sure that ma-crame has been invented many, many times, probably first using plant fibers. Perhaps sailors carried it to the greatest level of in-ventiveness during periods of uneventful passage on calm seas, the knots like an abacus marking the time and the miles of ocean.

Mrs. Wurlitzer heard of this knotting I was doing and asked
if I could refurbish some old lampshades that she was fond of.
So I had another chance to play around with constructing things
out of threads and enjoyed it thoroughly. They were gloriously
impractical projects—generous gestures on her part, really—but
she was probably able to use her favorite old clip-on bed lamp
for many more years after I rewove the fabric and relined it with
raw silk. Every now and then through the winter she came up
with some intriguing project for me; and later, when I was weaving in earnest, she also bought a large tapestry.

Jenny learned to walk that winter, and it was also the year in
which it became clear that Kimry had already become a craftswoman. Since she was very small she had made things, often
things requiring planning and some combining of materials. She
would come to one of us with a project in mind and if we said,
"Oh, I don't know if we have the stuff to do that," she would
counter with something like, "Oh yes we do. We can cut rings
out of this inner tube and then cut some wire and then . . . ,"
outlining the whole plan, so we were bound to help her; and
soon she needed very little help aside from the actual acquisition
of materials. She worked happily with most any materials and
ingeniously worked out joinings and fastenings that were both
functional and intriguing.

One evening we left the girls at home with a sitter and when
we returned, late, Jenny was asleep as we expected, but Kimry
was sitting up, finishing a project with the sitter. She had made—
of clay and wire and bits of cloth and cardboard—an elaborate
miniature carriage with wheels that turned. The sitter was fascinated, surprised that it was so late, and assured us that she would
be glad to come again any time we needed her.

Baby sitting fees were a great luxury that winter, however.
Usually the girls went visiting with us or people came to our
house; there was very little formal entertaining, or need for it.
We took them with us to openings of art exhibits and other public
events from the time they were very small, so they found these
perfectly normal everyday family activities. At the lowest winter
ebb financially—February—Oli got a job for a month as a bar-
tender at the Taos Inn, and that carried us through. There simply
weren't jobs to be had of an ordinary sort in Taos during those
years. It became rather a joke when we realized that one of the

only parlor games played on long winter evenings in Taos was "How to Make Money"—which implied, "without leaving town or giving up all one's working time."

Dinner parties were simple affairs. The classic menu was designed around beans—and, in fact, beans taste very differently as made by different cooks. My trick was to cook broccoli stems with them; it gave a subtle "green taste" that made them lighter without really changing their basic flavor. Also, it avoided the problem of how not to waste broccoli stems, and avoiding waste was more or less a design principle with us.

The Browns, Malcolm and Rachel, were characteristically busy during those early years. We had dinners together and became familiar with Rachel's special talent for, with apparently the greatest of ease, concocting gracious meals from the simplest ingredients on her black iron stove. Their large main room was a wonderful place to spend winter evenings, lit only by kerosene lamps and a roaring fire in the adobe fireplace. And we traded children back and forth for visits, but there was little *extra* time in their lives at that stage. They were busy with building their house—a mammoth undertaking—and then in the spring, with another friend, the writer Bob Grant, they put in a huge vegetable garden. We saw a lot of Kristina, though, who was of necessity on a freer schedule; we would often take off on the spur of the moment for a day-trip, exploring, or simply have long visits over coffee or supper.

Of course, the great dramatic event of that winter was the birth of Ian in February. Kristina went down to Santa Fe to wait for his arrival, and when we heard the news Rachel and I hurried down to see them. We weren't allowed to see Kristina in her hospital room for some reason. But we felt that it was important for her, so we somehow managed to get two white coats and in these disguises appeared in her room, to her utter delight. Bucky was there to see his son, the first time that I met him. Ian was a sweet little boy and quickly became part of things, of our gatherings and activities. Jenny enjoyed immensely having him around, and for Cousin Lorelei his appearance on February 27 was special as it was her second birthday.

The Craft House

Most projects involving a number of people are later recalled in as many ways and assigned varying degrees of importance. So it was with the Craft House. For Kristina it was one of the high points of living in Taos. For me, it was the beginning of weaving tapestries, something I had been working toward for years. When we recalled it with Rachel, however, her response was, "Oh, you mean the *first* Craft House." For her, *the* Craft House was the second one, years later, in Arroyo Seco. Actually, though, this first one would prove to be crucial to the new career that was about to become very important in Rachel's life as it provided her with a loom, "just in case" she ever wanted to weave, as Kristina put it.

Early in the spring Oli started looking for a larger studio space, and one day he came home, much excited, with news of a large empty building on a back street in Taos; and he took Kristina and me to see it. What he proudly showed us was a U-shaped hacienda-style adobe with a wall and arched gateway on the street, enclosing a patio. Within it, two apricot trees were just coming into bud, and a portal ran around the inner side of the building—an absolutely charming setting. It was a little neglected looking with leaves and trash piled in the corners, but to us the unused look was encouraging; we might be able to rent it.

Inside, there were several large rooms, perfect for workshops, as well as several smaller ones. Both we and Kristina had been cooped up in combined living-working spaces for the winter, and this incredibly grand building was far beyond any fantasy we had of a studio. We investigated immediately and were told that it was the old Vocational Building (built in the 1930s as part of a statewide program to revive the making of traditional Spanish crafts under the Works Progress Administration) and had stood empty over all the years since the WPA program had closed down. We had no difficulty getting permission to use it in return for repairs and maintenance.

We set right to work, cleaning and figuring out what repairs had to be done immediately. Our plans had changed from just a studio to a whole complex of work spaces. It was hard to believe that such a beautiful building was standing empty. Across most of the back of it was a long room with a fireplace in a corner, and Kristina and I immediately saw that as a weaving room. A small corner room beside it could become a sales shop if things went as we were now envisioning them. A big side room was perfect for Oli's studio and for exhibits, and across the courtyard were two more rooms in the other wing.

Out behind the building there was a shed where we looked for usable materials. Digging through the junk, we noticed some finished pieces of wood, and it gradually dawned on us what they were. Looms! We dug for more pieces and hauled everything that could possibly be a loom part into the big room and started sorting out the pieces. Hardly believing our luck, we put together *two* fine looms—for Kristina a large one for weaving standing up and for me a lovely, simple, light but strong sitting one. They were handmade, probably right in this building. The project was beginning to take on mythical proportions, and Kristina and I, particularly, felt that a new era was beginning. While Oli applied white paint to his studio, Kristina and I warped our looms and set up our materials in our respective corners of the workshop, Jenny and Ian happily playing in the midst of the activity.

Malcolm and Rachel came to see the place and immediately decided to join us and to build a long silk-screen printing table along one side of the workshop. In her last year of college at Radcliffe Rachel had decided to go into architecture, taking most of her classes at the Harvard Graduate School of Design; she loved it and made top grades, but when she applied for the architecture program GIs returning from the war had priority and she was not accepted. So she went to New York and took a job at the Metropolitan Museum in the catalog department (which had just received a Stieglitz collection including Georgia O'Keeffe's letters and other papers) and for the next two years worked there and studied at the Art Students' League and Cooper Union. Then she and a friend decided to leave the city for the West and new adventures, traveling by bus with all their belongings, bolts of cloth and textile paints to set up a silk-screen printing business in Colorado Springs. For a year they ran a little shop in the front of their live-in studio, where they designed and printed drapery material and had fashion shows of clothes made from their own printed cloth. So now she and Malcolm would set up a printing area in the new building and join us in making plans and getting things in shape.

We cleared the courtyard of an accumulation of dried leaves, freshened the wood trim with paint, repaired and washed windows, and soon felt quite thoroughly at home. Our total of six children had plenty of space to play and do their own projects. As we worked we tried to come up with a name for the place with no luck at all until one day Lorelei asked her mother if they were going in to work at "that *craft* house." It seemed to describe the place perfectly and the name stuck; The Craft House it was.

Work on the printing table was under way; I started weaving ponchos and stoles, and Kristina continued with her pillows and bags. Oli was at work in his studio and decided to teach a painting class for the summer.

We wanted to introduce ourselves officially to the community, and the Taos News announced that at our open house there would also be refreshments and music—Jenny Vincent playing the accordion and Hattie Trujillo the mandolin. Our first press release read, "The Craft House is designed to promote interest in local crafts by centralizing production and offering a sales outlet for the work produced. Weaving, silk screen printing, leathercraft, and woodwork are currently being done." It also announced that art and design classes would be held for local residents. The open house was a great success, with dancing in the patio late into the night.

I suppose that what we had created was a cooperative, since we shared the space, the costs, and the responsibilities, but we never thought to call it that. With the quantities of craft shops in and around Taos now it's hard to remember that then there were none, until Ed Bewley opened a design shop called Trends on the Plaza. Kristina sold pillows there and, later on, Kimry sold lampshades and mobiles. There were shops that showed fine old Spanish and Indian weaving, and also traditional Indian jewelry and other artifacts. But the contemporary craft movement simply had not come alive yet. Around the country there were individual craftpeople, or groups of them, doing skilled and beautiful work, but the popular movement had not begun.

Kristina must have been one of the first independent weavers to work in Taos, meaning independent of an inherited tradition. Perhaps that isn't accurate, either; she actually did inherit a tradition—she just didn't happen to be Spanish.

She had gone to Colorado University for two years after high school, with no particular career plans, then became interested in occupational therapy and went to Columbia University for three years of combined medicine and crafts courses—including jewelry, woodworking, and weaving on a small table loom. After college she got a job at the State Hospital in Las Vegas, New Mexico. There she found three looms with warps "tangled like spaghetti" and sat up nights straightening them all out so they could be used again, as the materials budget was practically non-existent. She began her weaving instruction with old hospital blankets cut into strips and gradually revived the weaving program, becoming thoroughly familiar with the workings of looms and, especially, learning to easily and quickly warp them. Then she moved across the mountains to Taos, where she worked for the Welfare Department for two years and, in her spare time, started weaving with the handspun wool yarn that was traditional there. She found women in the valley who still spun and were willing to sell some yarn—Virginia Lucero and her neighbor in Arroyo Seco, Mrs. Montaño.

When we set up our looms at the Craft House she shared those sources with me. I had not had a floor loom to weave on since leaving college, though I had from that time been sure that I would one day start weaving tapestries. Now, suddenly, I had a really lovely loom and a wonderful working space shared with friends. I could really start weaving in earnest, though it was still some months before I actually started my first tapestry.

The Craft House had an exciting summer. As we had hoped, it became a sort of cultural center, a place for exchange and for impromptu gatherings. We had poetry readings, musical evenings of various sorts, exhibitions of jewelry, photographs (Justin Locke and Walter Chappel), paintings—and Oli's art classes continued through the summer. Many of the gatherings were very spur-of-the-moment affairs. One of us would meet someone who was in town, perhaps only briefly, who had something interesting to contribute and offer them an invitation for an evening; we'd all get on the phone and spread the word and produce a small but appreciative audience.

Another important event for me that summer, along with finally acquiring a loom, was making a new and lifelong friend. Joan and Erik Erikson came to Taos for the summer on their way back from Mexico. Erik Erikson was one of the leading figures in the field of psychoanalysis and human development, the author of *Childhood and Society* and *Insight and Responsibility*. He was busy much of the time with work on his new book, *Young Man Luther,* and not involved in our activities except for parties (where he and Joan waltzed divinely), but Joan had time to be involved with the Craft House. We had a show of her jewelry and through the summer became fast friends.

Rachel and Malcolm finished their forty-foot-long printing table, but just in time for their housebuilding and gardening season out in Arroyo Seco to begin, so printing was put off until fall. Then Oli and I found a wonderful house to move to from the Wurlitzer Foundation, out on the Valdez rim beyond Arroyo Seco, in an area called Des Montes. It was a wonderful spot, close under the mountains crowned by Lobo Peak, looking down into the long valley called Valdez—partly village, partly farms, clustered on either side of the Rio Hondo, which emerged from the mountains at the head of the valley. We were happy to be in the country again and I, particularly, was torn between the workshop in town and my enjoyment of our new home.

Home finally won out, and we moved my loom to Des Montes; I knew that there would be a lot more time to weave there, where I could sit down to work for short periods between other activities. I was an early riser and in the long days of summer could get up at five and have a couple of hours of solitary work before the family woke and the busy day started. I really enjoyed blending weaving with other things; my idea of a perfect working day included some period of solitary work, then smaller pieces of casual time interspersed between household projects, walks later in the day, perhaps a visit at coffee time, constructing a stew or a soup in midday, and letting it simmer away as other things went on. There was for me something very rich and luxurious about a day put together in this fashion, and in this way I was able to do my own work and also be available for the girls.

For Kristina, however, the Craft House was still the perfect setting for work. She loved everything about it; it was the total opposite of the year she had just been through—isolated and lonely for much of the time. Here she was busy, working with people, and Ian was happy and safe, playing nearby as she worked. So my departure to weave at home seemed to her real abandonment; years later she told me that was one of the few times she was really angry with me. During the summer Virginia Mallory joined the group and took over the running of the selling shop; then we made the two rooms in front of that into a small apartment for her and her daughter, Angie. So toward the end of the summer Kristina and Virginia were the only ones working full time in the building.

Kristina invited Mrs. Montaño to bring some of the yarn she spun to the shop, and when she did she would often visit for the afternoon—sitting, sweet and dignified, speaking only Spanish, just being sociable and interested in what was going on. Kristina had taken me to visit her at her home in Arroyo Seco, and she had shown me her collection of beautiful rugs and blankets, spun and woven over her long lifetime. Kristina and I loved seeing them—the softness of the yarn, many of the colors a little muted by time. We were seeing our chosen career of weaving from another perspective in these pieces that Mrs. Montaño had kept out of all those that she had woven over the years. There is a bond between people who love handspun woolen yarn and, as I suppose happens in almost any discipline, to a beginner the person who has spent a lifetime in a medium and is experienced and expert in its handling has a special, almost awesome, quality. In Mrs. Montaño we found confirmation that working with handspun wool yarn was going to be a gratifying pursuit.

I had an intense visual involvement with this valley. It had become for me not simply a background, a setting in which I enjoyed living, but a kind of total experience, an environment in which my thoughts took place, a web of occurrences that seemed to have become connected with the very paths of my wonderings. Its visual intricacies became my focus, the focus for my interacting with the world.

Then one day I tacked tiny nails into the top and bottom of

an 8″ × 10″ frame of wood, strung linen thread around them, and with bits of leftover yarn and a comb I devised the way that I would construct tapestries. This first bit was miniaturized and crude, but in it I arrived at the method of building shapes that suited me—not only straight across the warp, but also with curves and slants where that seemed to be needed.

But it was finally Joan Erikson's doing, my weaving the first tapestry. One day she brought me a little bundle of handspun yarns—Mrs. Montaño's that she had bought at our shop—and asked me to weave her a tapestry with sunflowers in it, like those that were just then blooming over the valley, lining every road-side. The colors she brought were a little light blue, some shades of light natural brown, and some bright, warm yellow—sun-flower yellow.

I wove a sort of undulating ground, wove streaks of the blue into it here and there like bits of sky showing through, and then in the upper section wove in fairly realistic sunflowers with sep-arate, somewhat windblown-looking petals, and then when the yellow was all used up, finished the piece with the rest of the earthy brown. It was primitive but pleasing, and Joan was very happy with it—a bit of New Mexico to take back with her to New England. So that was the beginning. It was also the begin-ning of one of the most important friendships I would know, crucial in the turning points of my life, both creative and personal, over the thirty years to come.

Des Montes

S ummer in Des Montes was delightful. Our house was cool and roomy; in back, a paved and roofed patio extended the living space—a fine place from which to watch the afternoon rainstorms. Those were usually brief and vigorous, cooling and cleansing the air. They produced wonderful rainbows—from our house, usually with the mountain as backdrop. Often they were clear double bows and formed three-quarters of a circle—beginning on the flat top land, then rising into an arc that finally ended on the valley floor below, brilliant in color. Often, too, there would be dramatic cloud events after night storms. Sometimes in the early mornings the whole Valdez valley would be filled with a long cloud like a mammoth roll of carded wool, a vaporous submarine tethered to the side of the mountain. Then, when the first rays of morning sun cleared the peaks and struck it, the vapor would spring upward and disappear, consumed within a blue sky.

Our house sat in a grove of tall trees, just back from the edge of the ridge above the long valley-village of Valdez, and we looked across it to the mountains, crowned by Lobo Peak. At the head of the valley a rushing mountain stream, the Rio Hondo, emerged from Hondo Canyon, then traveled placidly through the valley, providing irrigation water as well as good fishing, through the smaller canyon at its end, on through to the village of Arroyo Hondo where it was used for irrigation throughout that valley and eventually dropped again, into the Rio Grande.

The rim road jogged in front of our house to cross the ditch, then continued on the very brink, looking over the valley some four hundred feet below. This was a wonderful walk—adobe houses and compounds beside the road and far below us a miniaturized pattern of fields divided by hedgerows and occasional houses led to by tiny roads around the fields. The Rio Hondo's course through the valley showed as a meandering band of trees down its length. If we walked far enough, the land began to fall away toward the desert in the west, and late in the afternoon we could watch the sun sink beyond the far blue mountain line, then walk home watching the last color play on our mountains. Oli and Kimry flew kites from the rim out over the valley and when the air currents were just right, could watch them diving around *below* where they stood.

Valdez was a study in the illusion of levels. It appeared to be a reasonably flat-floored valley divided into more or less level fields and orchards and pastures. The river flowed down its middle and a road skirted the side next to the mountain, then turned and crossed the valley and climbed the near valley wall, to emerge at the edge of the ridge just in front of the house where we lived, where it met the rim road.

Just in front of our house the ditch flowed under a small bridge. The odd thing was that from that little bridge one could look far down to the head of the valley below, to where that ditch was diverted from the Rio Hondo just as it emerged from the mountain canyon. Although the head of the valley certainly *appeared* to be far below us—since the water obviously ran *down* to us, we knew that, contrary to all appearances, the wide-floored valley must gradually slope downward. And our ridge, which seemed to be quite flat when driving or walking along it, was actually a gradual rise toward the mountains. Even from the road on the far side of the valley it was hard to read the ditch-path as almost level and the rim above as rising, the ditch *seemed* to be going uphill and the ridge to be flat. Finally we discovered that the various lines could be believed when seen framed by a car window from that road. It was a puzzle that we enjoyed—an illusion so strong that it continued to function even when the facts were grasped.

Under the trees in front of our house the ditch seemed to become an ordinary stream; the bank under the trees was grassy and violets grew there. We dug up lovely blue columbines from the bank of the stream up the canyon and planted them at home where they were refreshed, still, by the same waters, only many miles later. It was a wonderfully cool place on hot summer days, and the children often retreated there.

Another virtue of this new establishment of ours was a small orchard way out in back. The first tree was a mulberry, a tree that I think of as the friend of children, having known one when small—shady, branches spreading enough to make room for several children, and wonderful fruit that ripened so gradually that keeping it eaten occupied several summer weeks and created an intimate relationship of sorts with birds. At the tree I once knew well, there was a shrieking of birds (were they jays?) when my brothers and I approached, and they would kite in and out of the high branches and watch us warily and, we thought, greedily. In New Mexico jays are magpies and they and Kimry and her friends were like rival gangs alternately occupying a territory. I remember, too, the lovely red stains mulberries produced—witness of pleasure.

Beyond that were pear, plum, and apricot trees, each wonderful in its own way. We arrived too late to witness the blooming that year; fruit was well under way. The orchard grass was an unruly, rich tangle, keeping its green after much other wild growth had begun to turn dry. Children always find flowers, and the ones who gathered at our house that summer periodically brought me bouquets of the latest discoveries. One of the favorites was a wild (or gone wild) pea that appeared around the edges of yards, roads, ditches, and pastures with magenta-purple bonnet-like blooms. On the hottest days we would see Kimry, surrounded by other children and little heaps of blooms, sitting on the grassy bank of the stream in the shade, inventing things to make out of flowers and leaves.

I think the southwestern child must have a special comprehension of light and shade, the contrast there is so great. In my memory of childhood in Texas, outdoor sheltered corners seemed dramatically significant. One could walk across acres of field and arrive at a corner fencepost where grass grew tall and perhaps some scrub or sapling plant had grown, in that protected setting, tall enough to sit under, and there retreat from the presence of space and look inward to rest for a while. Years later, when I spent many years in the East, I would sometimes feel that I was in a *featureless* landscape—that there was no opportunity to *measure space*. It seemed that space was so decorated with growing things that it had no particular shape or dimension. When I first lived in the East, at college in North Carolina, I luxuriated in the richness, marveled at the intricacy of unfamiliar plant forms; their arrangement in the landscape seemed garden-like, so gracefully designed. But it was not a reality that I could live with forever.

So the summer passed. Oli was at work in his studio with windows looking across the valley to the pinon-speckled mountainside. I found plenty of time to weave between the various things going on. We all took part in the special events at the Craft House and Oli continued his art classes there, but only Kristina and Virginia really worked there.

For me it was a wonderful period. Finally I was beginning to weave tapestries as I had intended for so long and I loved it. Without any conscious planning as to a way of working, I had begun to construct weavings that had the feel of the landscape in them and, also, from then on I worked with homespun yarn. Kristina shared her local sources with me, and we found enough, somehow, to keep us both weaving. Early in the fall Oli and I and some friends made a two-week trip into the Navajo country, and at a remote trading post I bought a few balls of a lovely, warm, earth-colored handspun yarn. In my innocence I imagined it came from a sheep of that color, but when I skeined and washed the yarn, to my dismay all of the lovely color fell into the water, leaving a pure white yarn. It was still beautiful—soft and very evenly spun—and I treasured it, remembering the space and lovely loneliness of the desert country where I bought it. Occasionally we were able to buy brown or gray homespun, but usually it was white, and I began to dye colors, using the Putnam dyes that I was familiar with from the old days of belt-making. With each piece that I wove, ideas for more presented themselves.

Then in the fall Kristina took a teaching job in Special Education in the Taos school system, working with retarded children. She and Ian moved into town into a friend's house, and she found a wonderful Ian-sitter—Lena, who became a sort of devoted aunt to him. Then Rachel also got a job as a caseworker with the Welfare Department. Kimry and the Brown boys were back in school and usually Rachel dropped Lorelei and her tricycle off at our house in the morning, and she and Jenny spent their days happily playing together. The Craft House was closed down for the winter; we would see later how the next summer's plans would go.

Depending on the rainfall through the summer as well as the snowpack of the previous winter, the larger valley either stayed green longer or turned brown earlier. The color of the turning leaves was most distinctively yellow—aspen on the mountains and cottonwoods tracing the courses of streams across the broad valley, with small isolated trees standing out here and there like perfect golden brush strokes. If the mountains received much snow during a winter, the ditches would flow long and abundantly in the summer and several rich, green harvests of alfalfa could be made. If not, water for the fields would become scarce and have to be jealously parceled out, used by each farmer carefully for the time apportioned him.

On our walks along the rim road we watched the colors turn gradually in the valley below and saw the great aspen groves on Lobo turn gold. Then the snows came and Valdez took on still another aspect. Right after a storm there was pristine simplicity— just snow-roofed houses and fence or hedgerow lines. Then tracks would begin to appear as farm animals moved about the fields and farmers' vehicles relocated the roads. Every day the tracks would thicken, crossing and re-crossing each other in elaborate patterns. Then we noticed that some of them passed right through fences and realized that these were made by deer, come down from the foothills to browse. Just after a heavy storm the mountains were almost entirely white. Then, gradually, wind and the weight of the snow would free the evergreens and the slopes were again dotted with dark green for most of the way up, the remaining swaths of white covering areas of rock face or the meadows above the treeline. This was for us a new sort of vantage point for witnessing winter, closer to the mountains and their weather; the close and far views out of our windows in all directions made a lovely backdrop for our days.

Winter was also a wonderful time for working, and I began to think of fall as the real beginning of the year. The pleasant sociabilities of summer would diminish as visitors left. The very air became different—clearer, more buoyant—and with the first frost it would become almost visible in its clarity. There was a particular kind of quiet with those fall days, as though with the end of the growing time all was resting and still. Winter stretched ahead as a dimension of time for working, a simplicity after the flamboyance of summer, a splendid isolation.

Tapestries

Through that first fall and winter of weaving tapestries, I became more skilled in achieving the results I wanted with the particular technique that I had arrived at for working. The process was proving to be an intensely exciting exploration, full of surprising discoveries. This valley that had become my visual home and the larger spaces beyond it where we occasionally traveled fed my eyes and my mind with more images and puzzles than I could ever weave or unravel.

The tapestries were primarily about the landscape, and with the freedom of this technique I had adopted, I could explore the intricacies of the space and forms and colors that I saw around me. In a way, I was weaving the *activity* of what I saw—the mysterious ways in which a bit of shadow would seem to become a form where it lay across a vast stretch of desert floor, or how distant mountain peaks would appear to become blended when their inclines were thrown into similar shadow at some particular time of day. I didn't try to weave these specific physical events; I simply watched them and they became part of my visual vocabulary, experiences from which to draw when I began to weave a tapestry. I built the tapestries line by line out of this handspun thread that seemed so willing to form for me these spaces, these illusions, these ambiguities and the beautiful mysteries that were played out in this landscape with every change in time of day or season of the year or shift in the weather. It seemed quite natural to let the lines of my weaving flow as I focused on bits of phenomena and then sat at my loom and wove my response to them.

Though the Putnam dyes that I was using came in something like fifty-six different shades, I found that I still needed to mix colors. When making up colors for a tapestry that was taking shape in my mind, I needed a number of gradations of a color in order to be able to bring the color in, play it up, relate it to the next color, and then often echo it somewhere in the piece. I would try to dye the color as I saw it in my mind's eye, then work to get one a little warmer, a little bluer, and so on. I would often discover that my mental sketch was too simple, that I was only seeing the high points and that the actual accomplishing of what was in my mind required some spacing colors, some leavening that would allow the other colors to function freely.

Gradually I worked into a system of dyeing up a batch of yarns in the colors that seemed to be what I would need, then beginning to weave, and stopping to dye more when I figured out what was missing. Beginning a new tapestry was a curious process. Sometimes the idea that I began with was simply a sense of some direction in which I wanted to go. Perhaps a color or a particular kind of line would stick in my mind, and I would set off in pursuit of it. I would dye a few colors that seemed capable of carrying me in the right direction and try to begin weaving some space in which my idea or curiosity could take shape. Early on, I learned that this beginning space was important, that I must resist the temptation to begin finalizing things too soon, that I must very slowly approach the visual image that I was after. In a sense I had to first make a place in which it could happen, almost weave in premonition of what was going to happen, a process that also served to keep the image or goal suspended in my mind long enough for it to take on more concrete form.

Tapestry weaving, of course, has the built-in difficulty that painting hasn't; you must begin at one end and go to the other. It's the nature of the craft. You can't begin with your basic idea and then move around it to further refine or elaborate it in any direction. I could occasionally remove a bit of color and substitute something else with a hook or needle, but generally I had to commit myself to a direction and stay with it, recognizing a mistake before it was surrounded and couldn't be removed.

I was attracted to the idea of using natural dyes as being in tune with the natural yarn that I used and did so sometimes out of curiosity. Generally, though, this didn't suit my way of working. To accomplish my particular results it was absolutely necessary to have many shades—warmer, cooler, bluer, redder—of the color that I was interested in. This would have been very difficult with natural dyes—first of all, very time consuming. But mostly it was that different colors came from things that were indigenous to geographically different areas. The natural dyes had the reputation of being subtler, but I felt that the quality of harshness usually associated with commercially-dyed yarns was usually the result of a limited palette rather than intrinsically poor color quality. Though groups of naturally dyed yarns are often lovely combinations, I found them no more so than the colors I made by combining the dye powders from by little brown Putnam packages. Color is color, and one must find the means to get colors that will work, be able to select or create them, and to use them effectively. I think that commercial dyeing has been unfairly blamed for a lot of poor color selection and combining. If weavers are given, or select, a limited palette they will have limited choice, and it will take a combination of talents, in design as well as placement, to make these colors subtle, or even to make them work at all. The lovely old soft-colored Rio Grande blankets were often originally not soft-colored at all, but have become so through years of use and exposure to light. If you poke apart the threads in a pale rose section of one of these blankets you will often discover a quite bright red-rose where the yarn has lain in shadow all those years.

Sometimes I dyed up a color that was very difficult to use. Once I dyed a large skein of a strong middle-rose color and tried over and over again to put it into a tapestry with other colors that seemed sympathetic, but it simply wouldn't work. It looked heavy and lifeless no matter what I put it next to—it seemed to have no personality at all; it didn't do a thing. I finally decided to design a tapestry around it, to find a way to make it work. It was against my principles to brand a color as *no good*. The solution proved to be dyeing colors close to it, but in several progressively lighter shades. With these I isolated the color, building up to it gradually with a narrow space of the slightly lighter shade. *Then* I found that I could introduce the strong colors with which it could get along—in this case, quite strong orange-golds. It needed bold brightness to relate to, but there needed to be a neutral line between these bold, strong colors. It worked, and the strong rose could be seen as a good color in itself, relating comfortably with other strong colors when a successful bridge was made between them.

One of the most useful discoveries that I made was the value of having *slight* colors. These were colors that I dyed with so little dye powder that there was more an *impression* of color than color itself, and they became indispensable to me. When wanting lightness—an area of space—I sometimes found that pure white didn't work, that it failed to give the feeling of unoccupied space that I needed. I found that just the smallest drift of color on the yarn made it work. In many situations white became too opaque, and adding just the slightest bit of blue dye that I could manage turned it to a much more transparent space and seemed to breathe air into the work. I used tints of gold or gray for this, too, but the most useful was this bit of middle blue. It seemed the most neutral, the most reflective foil for other colors. Someone told me that it was like mixing a bit of Prussian Blue pigment into white paint to give a more *alive* quality to white walls.

This dyeing of yarns was a little like making soup, which I also loved, beginning in the morning with bones for broth and tasting and adding other elements throughout the day as I worked at my loom. I never became a skilled dyer, versatile with different types of dyes or working with the range of technical possibilities as Rachel later did, but it became one of the most delightful parts of the tapestry process for me. Usually I didn't dye and weave on the same day as I found that my eyes were so influenced by the intense experience of following the colors that they needed a rest to be able to begin arranging them in the actual work. I found that if I went right to work I tended to weave as though I had already used colors that had been experienced in the dyepot rather than in the tapestry. It was grand, though, to wake up in the morning knowing that a whole raft of colored skeins had dried during the night and were waiting for me.

Rachel had not yet felt any special interest in weaving. Her life was busy in general with the continuing work on her house, and now she also had a full-time job, so the loom parts from the Craft House were simply stored in a corner. But this interest was about to surface. The loom was drawing her, and she saw the homespun yarn that Kristina and I were becoming so devoted to. Every day when she brought or picked up Lorelei she saw what I was doing and how I loved it. Finding enough yarn was still difficult for Kristina and me, though she had gotten some other women to take up spinning again. I assumed that at some point I would find a spinning wheel and begin making my own yarn.

Then a wonderful new yarn source appeared. I heard of Paula Simmons, a former weaver who had become totally involved in the spinning of yarn. She and her husband moved to the country in Washington and started raising sheep of as many colors as they could find or breed. After shearing they would spread out the fleeces and, separating the parts with variations in color, give the name of that sheep to the main color that it produced. So the sample cards for the yarns she spun were labeled with names of sheep rather than with color names. I ordered a group of colors— carefully, as they were very special and expensive—and used them all at once to weave a narrow vertical tapestry that looked like a receding series of eroded cliffs viewed through a narrow window. The yarns were wonderful natural shades of grays and browns, from pale to rich, and were great fun to work with. It was the first time that I, and Rachel as well, had seen such a range of natural colors and realized the subtle variations that could be achieved by mixing in the carding rather than in the dyepot, something with which we would both soon become deeply involved.

At some point during that winter Kristina discovered our first more or less unlimited source of handspun wool yarn—Mayatex Yarns in El Paso, Texas. The yarn came in long cocoon-like rolls and changed our lives; finally we had access to all we needed. Now I could dye up larger quantities of yarn and begin to build up a small supply of colors. Kristina, in her little rented house in town, was finding time to weave along with her teaching job and wove her first tapestry that winter. I still remember it—not in detail, but a bold, clear quality that it had. It had very simple shapes, just in black, brown, and white. I think that it had a very similarly dramatic quality to the intensely colorful pieces that her work has evolved to now, thirty years later.

In the spring a friend brought a visitor from the East to our house—Lenore Tawney, a well-known weaver whose work I had admired, and she suggested that I send slides of my tapestries to her agent in Chicago. This introduction to Marna Johnson, who handled the work of many people who worked in some textile form, was the beginning of a working friendship which lasted for the rest of Marna's life. Over the years she placed tapestries and arranged a number of commissions for me; she was a well-loved agent for many people during her career.

Spinning Wheels

The winter of 1958–59 turned out to be an important one. I finally got a spinning wheel and, finally, there were three of us—three weavers. Rachel remembers vividly the event that finally brought her to realize that she *must* weave. It was a show of traditional Spanish Rio Grande weaving at the Museum of International Folk Art in Santa Fe, beautiful blankets and rugs of indigo and white and natural black wool, finely woven of very lustrous yarn. She responded with a typical meteoric surge of energy, determination, and devotion. She and Malcolm pulled the bundle of loom parts out of the corner and put her first loom together—completely backwards at first, she recalls.

My spinning wheel, sent by friends, Mary and John Collier, from California, arrived dismantled, just a box of well-worn parts made of lovely tawny-gold old wood, with instructions to "tune it like a lute" until the various joinings were of the correct tightness. Kristina, Oli, and I, none of whom had been this close to a spinning wheel before, set about putting it together. Most of the parts showed some logical relationship to each other, but even so, putting them together correctly proved to be very tricky. Then, finally, I had a brilliant thought and dashed into the girls' room and found Jenny's copy of *Snow White and Rose Red* and there, realistically rendered, were pictures of a spinning wheel. With their help we managed to insert and connect everything in the proper way so that finally the whole became stable. When we figured out the path of the string, the wheel went round at the bidding of the treadle and this turned the bobbin. It was an impressive, intricate mechanism. There were a lot of false starts and fumblings before we could actually coerce it to make thread, but finally we got the hang of some of its subtleties and were able to actually spin some yarn.

Rachel and Malcolm decided to build their own spinning wheel. They had seen one that Alice Parrott, a nationally known Santa Fe weaver, had, the wheel of which was an ordinary bicycle wheel, and took off from that. By the heat of the fireplace Malcolm bent a slim strip of wood into a wheel, and then, from an old generator part, made a long spindle that turned smoothly on ball bearings. It was a lovely object and worked beautifully— quite a feat for two people who didn't know how to spin.

Now we needed raw wool to work with and it was some months before shearing time, so Kristina and I decided to go wool gathering. We drove through all the dirt roads where we thought flocks of sheep might have been herded and, sure enough, there were little tufts of wool caught in the barbs of wire fences and bits clinging to fenceposts along the roads. We took this treasure of fiber home and I spun it up, one of the most satisfying lengths of yarn that I ever produced. At that stage we saw and thought wool all the time—suddenly clouds seemed often to be shaped like well-carded whorls of perfectly clean white wool.

Rachel's job territory at that time was around Costilla, north of Taos, a sheep-raising area. As she talked with her clients, she found herself gazing over their shoulders at their flocks, looking especially for brown sheep, which she was surprised to discover were often black ones with sun-bleached tips to their wool. She brought home batches of wool, all dirty and covered with ticks, and spent long evenings happily carding it. She got a fellow caseworker, Dolores Montoya, who knew how to spin on the *malacate,* the Spanish handspindle, to help her and together they translated the spinning on the malacate to the horizontal arrangement of her wheel. Dolores had been very active in the revival of Hispanic weaving in New Mexico. The malacate is about a foot long (much larger than the South American handspindles, which are for spinning finer yarn) and spins the medium yarn traditional in Spanish-American weaving. My Swedish wheel worked on a different principle than these open-spindled wheels, and was actually designed for making finer yarn than I made with it.

Finally I found a farmer who had a sack of wool left from last year's shearing that he was willing to sell, and I began to spin in earnest. Gradually my yarn lost its nubby character and began to more correctly resemble a soft, springy, spiraling cylinder—evenly fluffy, without so many unspun sections resulting from the turning of the wheel getting ahead of my fingers' manipulation of the roll of carded wool.

So as it happened, Rachel on her newly designed wheel and I on my old Swedish one began spinning a type of yarn that is almost precisely the same as the medium-weight, single-ply yarn that had been spun for two hundred years in the villages along the Rio Grande. Most likely this was largely because it was the kind of yarn we saw in the local Spanish weaving, the traditional Rio Grande blankets, and the lovely *Colcha* embroideries.

Spinning simply fascinates some people and intrigues others not at all. Rachel and I loved it. It was immensely satisfying to cause this soft, lively fiber to wind its way into yarn. I had never understood before that *yarn* was the name for an almost miraculous process: the twining of soft, warmth-holding fibers into a certain arrangement—a spiraling twist—that would *keep* them there so that they could be made into the myriad forms of textiles.

On our walks along the Valdez rim we had become acquainted with an elderly man of the neighborhood who got into the habit of dropping in to visit and check on the progress of our work. He liked Oli's bright, clear paintings and was interested to see what he would do next. When I began spinning, he offered to show me how to card wool properly, saying he had carded for his mother's spinning when he was a boy.

So we sat down to work and he immediately said, "Ahh—you're crowding the wool on the cards. You can't comb it out right that way." He patiently demonstrated, taking a small handful of wool and letting the wire hooks on the cards pull off just the right amount to work with. Then he combed the cluster of fibers with the second comb until they lay neatly in one direction amongst the wire teeth.

"See!" He would hold the card out for my inspection and, with a flourish, comb the wool free of the hooks, rolled into a small, fluffy whorl that he pronounced, "Perfect!" We worked by the fireplace in the corner of the living room, and when we began he set a small pile of raw wool on the hearth where the warmth would soften the lanolin in it, making it *willing* to be spun. When I pick up my cards to work, I will forever remember this sweet old man sitting patiently with me by the fire, showing me *good* carding.

Then one day he brought me a present, a number of large balls of indigo-dyed homespun made years ago by his grandmother. The outer layers of the yarn were slightly mottled where the exposed parts had faded a little. Indigo homespun is very special. The other natural-dyed colors are beautiful but somehow understandable, as we see those colors in plants and woods and lichens and earth. But to be able to make a blue, natural color is like borrowing from the visible but intangible color of the sky, of distance, of large bodies of water—things that you cannot pick up.

The yarn was perfectly preserved, with not a sign of moths ever having set foot in it; later, I wished I had asked him how it had been safely stored for those many years. When I wound it into skeins in order to wash and refresh it, it proved to be mostly two shades—one a pure middle classic indigo and the other much darker, almost a navy blue. I decided to weave the lighter color into a small, special tapestry and hung the skeins up where I could look at them and start imagining what shape they would take.

The darker yarn I made into a jacket, weaving the fronts and back across in one piece, carefully weaving in the slits for the armholes so that I wouldn't have to cut them later. Shoulder seams were necessary, and when they were done I cast the stitches for knitting the sleeves directly into the woven armhole edge. The final touch for this one-of-a-kind garment was an accidentally invented stitch for adding width to the front edges. I tried knitting, but it wasn't right—then crocheting, which didn't work either. I thrust the crochet hook in once more, then pulled it out in disgust halfway through the stitch and there, lo and behold, was an entirely new stitch, perfect for this edging, in appearance halfway between knitting and crocheting. With it I worked the fronts and collar and it looked, finally, very all-of-a-piece and worthy of this special yarn.

In the spring of 1959 Rachel left her Welfare Department job to be at home for the summer. She was spinning yarn to weave on her new loom and began her first piece of weaving, remembered fondly as "just a beautiful, beautiful, soft traditional Rio Grande style weaving." She recalled vividly to me years later,

I was just obsessed! I was just praying to God that I
wouldn't die before I had a chance to weave. I had so many

*ideas, things that I wanted to do. I had seen the things you
and Kristina were doing and I had worked with textiles and
done some kind of art work all my life, but I had never been
so excited about anything before.*

That fall the Brown family moved to Colorado where Malcolm had a teaching job at the Rocky Mountain School in Carbondale, and Rachel's loom went with them. She acquired a weaving book—Mary Black's *Key to Weaving*—and remembers that she had just had a wisdom tooth out, which permitted her to curl up with the book, reading it "like a mystery novel," absolutely fascinated. She set herself up as a weaving teacher at the school, keeping barely one jump ahead of her students that first year. Also, she found an old book on handcraft techniques that told how to set up a Navajo loom; she put one up in their house "in order to weave wide and big" and, on that, wove rugs and tapestries, using the Craft House loom for fabrics. Then she bought a four-harness Swedish loom and on that could try out the more complicated techniques that had intrigued her so in Mary Black's book. By the time they returned to Taos, she had three years of learning and teaching behind her and was utterly involved in her new weaving career. Now, all these years later, I think that for all of us it is hard to think of Rachel without being conscious of her identity as weaver. She is a textile person, through and through, and over the years has pored into one after another aspect of the craft with never-ending curiosity and devotion.

Joan carding wool.

. . . and spinning yarn.

*Photographs on pages 55–58
by Mildred Tolbert.*

. . . and weaving a tapestry.

Rachel working with a hand carding machine.

. . . and spinning.

. . . and tying a new warp onto her loom.

LEFT: *Kristina displaying weavings.*
BOTTOM: *Kristina weaving in her Arroyo Seco house.*

Productive Years

The year after Rachel and her family moved to Colorado we moved across the valley again, to the Este Es Ranch. Our house was an old adobe, the original one on the property; it was separated by an orchard from a large, somewhat newer one that had, many years before, been the headquarters for a guest ranch. Ours was el-shaped, like a bent New York railroad flat, one room wide and thick-walled, with deep window sills and pleasant shaded views into the orchard on one side, then open across farms toward the south.

This house had been very little modernized aside from the addition of plumbing and electricity, and we enjoyed its old and settled feeling. To move into a traditional Spanish adobe house is to become enveloped in the culture in a very tangible way, in a sculptural, graceful extension of the earth itself. It was very different from homes we had experienced elsewhere, both simpler and more aesthetic, with an elegance that corresponded to the intricate simplicity of the landscape itself. These houses were a product of handcraft, were the shaping, in fact, of the landscape into a private dwelling, both a bringing indoors of the ineffable landscape and a sheltering from its largeness, from the brilliance of light, the length and coldness of the winters, from the winds of March. I think that one cannot adopt such an architecture, which is a blend of other cultures, without gaining a considerable sense of respect and association and sympathy with the cultures that produced it.

A portal ran along the inner side of the ell and, in the patio that gradually evolved there, I made my first flower garden: a riot of portulaca in a long hollowed-out log along one side and on the other a long bed of zinnias and snapdragons, pansies, and nasturtiums. This garden, where even annual flowers volunteered for each new summer of the five years we lived there, bred my urge for a true perennial garden which, expecting always to be making another move, I never quite dared to start. In the summers this was a lovely outdoor living room, then every fall we stacked wood high under the roof of the portal for our adobe corner fireplace and the wood stoves with which we heated our little stretched-out house. On sorties out into the country we collected stones with which to gradually pave the patio; often I would take whatever children were on hand for a picnic, driving out into the sagebrush land between the ranch and the foothills where they loved to collect rocks and flowers to take back home.

To the south, dirt roads led toward Rio Chiquito, following the irrigation ditches beside small adobe houses and farm fields, so we had again a variety of terrains for walking. There were corrals and other ranch outbuildings and in one old adobe Oli set up a painting studio, where he would develop his series of beautiful ellipse paintings. Later Kimry acquired a horse and it occupied, through the winter, one of the long-empty corrals and the adjoining small log barn.

It was a good house for living and working. I had plenty of time for weaving in between household activities and was beginning to show and to sell my work, usually from home; there still weren't galleries in Taos interested in showing weaving. I had entered tapestries in the Craftsmen of New Mexico exhibits at the wonderful Museum of International Folk Art in Santa Fe and had received awards several years, then in 1962 had a one-woman show of tapestries at the Bolles Gallery in San Francisco and the following year at the Kendall Gallery in San Angelo, Texas. In 1964 I wove a large tapestry, a commission from Victor Gruen Associates for a shopping center in the Los Angeles area, and sold a tapestry to Georg Jensen in New York. Usually, though, the sales were to individuals who weren't active collectors but happened to see something that spoke to them and often would need to pay for a piece gradually. Usually they returned for another tapestry later, or sent friends to see me when they came through Taos.

As I found better-quality fleeces to work with I developed a shortcut spinning method that turned out to be a great asset. I simply spread out bunches of fleece to warm—either outdoors or, in the winter in a sunny window or near the stove—and spun the wool directly, without carding.

It was a pleasant way of working and produced very special yarn. If there was some color variation in the fleece—say, lighter brown on the outer tips of a dark brown fleece—this color would show as an orderly twining through the yarn, rather than becoming evenly mixed as would result from thorough carding. But the discovery that I really enjoyed was that in spinning plain white wool, this method also produced a result in the dyeing afterward. When I spun directly from the sheared fleece, I discovered that the cut ends of the wool, from next to the sheep's body, took the dye differently from the outer tips so that by spinning without stirring up the wool by carding, these ends of the fibers fell into a sort of spiral pattern in the yarn and, when I dyed this yarn with a pale gold or very light blue, using very little dye, the result was a slightly varicolored yarn, which I found very useful in weaving tapestries; it provided a light, neutral color that was not quite opaque.

Later, Rachel told me that she taught this way of spinning that I happened upon to her apprentices at the Craft House and in her spinning workshops as a means of speeding up the yarn-making process, telling her students that "if you work with a good fleece you don't have to go through all this carding business." Of course, now, much spinning is done from precarded wool, which is also a wonderful shortcut, though I still find working with a fine natural fleece with all its lanolin still there the most delightful form of spinning; the fibers spring so willingly into yarn.

Jenny started school in Taos, where Kimry now was in high school. A family with four children moved into the other house, and the orchard and our house became a center of children's activities. Kimry took up the raising of mice and constructed elaborate cages for them in the kitchen, supervising the lives of generations of delicate white mice. Later the mice were replaced for a while by rabbits, and we even acquired a raccoon. One day in Taos Jenny and several other children waited in the car while I went into a store, and suddenly Jenny burst into the store to tell me that an Indian man in a pickup next to them had a little raccoon that he would sell for two dollars. "Couldn't we please buy it?" Of course we did and it became a beloved pet, sleeping each night on one of the girls' pillows, involving itself in all of the activities of the household, a thoroughly charming creature. Unfortunately, being on a friendly basis with our dog, it unwarily wandered into the path of a strange one and was killed, a very sad day.

Kimry's deft hands and eyes were busy with a variety of projects those days. She made tiny pieces of furniture and miniature quilts for Jenny's dolls, a 'Tittlemouse House" for her in a corner of the kitchen, with shelves for her papers and nails on which to hang her collection of necklaces and strings of beads; she was learning to write and from this corner could check letters out on food labels on the kitchen shelves.

Oli's work was going well. He was producing glorious color paintings and was busy with art activities in Taos, part of the Taos Moderns group. He was usually away for parts of those summers, teaching at the University of New Mexico and other colleges in the area. Kimry conducted an art workshop for about six younger children for several weeks that summer, and in another small adobe building behind our house we had a show of my tapestries one weekend, with Jenny and assistants serving punch and lemonade outside in the sun.

The kitchen of this house was large enough for many activities, with a long trestle table with benches where we could spread out projects or feed any number of people. It was there that we began a tradition of making and icing cookies with which to decorate our tree at Christmas. It happened that a number of artist friends dropped by on the first cookie baking day and they all helped, creating flying angels and surprising animals and decorations. After that we made them every year, though one Christmas Eve slipped up on us, and we decided to have an ordinary tree until we discovered that it didn't look at all right and hurriedly made up dough and baked and iced late into the evening, finally dropping into bed with our tree properly hung with bright cookies.

During these years we only saw Kristina during the summers. One winter she and Ian spent in the Bahamas where she taught a one-room school, then the following one they spent in a very different environment—Vermejo Park, a vast ranch in northeast New Mexico, where again she taught all the grades of a one-room school, this time for the children of ranch employees. Before the snow was too deep we visited her there and saw her tiny wooden schoolhouse set in the midst of this isolated ranchland. Occasionally they would get away for a few days in Taos, but for several years I was the only one of us actually living in the valley.

Then the Browns returned from Colorado and Kristina got a job at a small new private school in Taos, Cañoncito, where we also enrolled Kimry. Rachel and Malcolm worked on their house through the summer, but by fall Rachel had made her first big weaving plan—she would go into business weaving blankets. In Colorado she had woven double-width blankets, seventy-two inches wide on her thirty-six-inch loom, and would now weave double-face blankets using her own spun wool and mohair yarn, brushing the mohair on one side into a soft froth of color.

One day that winter Oli and I drove out to see them, in a celebratory mood as Oli had sold a small painting. When we arrived, Malcolm had just finished brushing a golden mohair blanket, fresh from Rachel's loom. It was a truly beautiful piece of weaving—natural brown and white on one face and soft, springy, gold mohair on the other—all Rachel's spinning. Oli, without mentioning our painting sale, said, "Let's buy it!" After we explained our sudden affluence, they told us that just before we arrived Malcolm had grandly held up the blanket and announced that the first person who saw it was going to buy it, then had groaned when he saw that it was only us at the door. I still have that blanket—twenty-six years old now and still a grand textile. Those years were very lean ones for all of us, when we lived primarily on "lack of expenses" as one friend put it; small windfalls were usually occasions for celebration. At about that time an interesting institution evolved amongst us—the "Fifty-dollar Floating Fund." Kristina recalls it as having been started by Oli, probably after some unexpected painting sale. He loaned the money to someone, and when they had recovered somewhat, financially, they passed it on to someone else who was at a low ebb, and it simply kept going.

Kristina left for one more winter, spending it in San Francisco where she began seriously weaving pillows and bags to sell. Then in the summer she and Rachel took a booth in the Albuquerque Arts and Crafts Fair, for which they won first prize that year and the two following ones. Kristina remembers that this gave her much more courage as a weaver.

The year 1965 was an important one for all three of us. That summer Rachel and Kristina decided to start another Craft House. They rented an old store building in Arroyo Seco, with shelves along the walls and plenty of space for setting up looms. So finally the Craft House lived again, the one that was to be so important for Rachel. Rachel recalls that it began as a result of Kristina's continual impulse to find places or situations in which weaving projects could happen. The building in Arroyo Seco was for sale, and she learned that a friend, Fred Fair, was interested in buying it, so they got together and arranged to rent it even before the purchase was accomplished. They opened just before Christmas and did a land office business through the holidays. Originally they were a group of five women—two weavers, a mask-maker, and two woodworkers—but before long three of them withdrew, and the cooperative became a partnership, with Rachel and Kristina sharing the managing and shop-sitting.

The old hardware store transformed beautifully into a craft shop, the shelves and glass-faced showcases quickly filling with rich-colored and textured textiles. Rachel continued to weave her mohair-faced blankets and spreads and developed garment designs also—ponchos and ruanas, for which she dyed up her own colors. Kristina wove pillows in her distinctive bright colors and lush rugs in her favorite heavy yarns.

Kimry had become a quite capable craftswoman by this time, constructing beautiful tissue-papier-mâché lampshades and mobiles and earrings of various materials, which she had sold at shops in Taos. Rachel's sons, Seth and Kinlock, had also begun making their first jewelry, and the three of them put their work in the new shop, so the next generation of artisans was beginning to function. Jenny and Lorelei, then just ten and eleven, would also become skilled silversmiths, but had not yet thought of such things. Their new adventure at that point was starting to take ballet lessons with Bette Winslow.

For me, the importance of that year was the birth of my son Conor. The first tapestry that I wove after he was born I named *Connery Pie*. It was designed to catch his eye, with sections of bright hot pink and of white, each with a simple shape within it—one, a rising sun. It's one of the few that I have from those years, though when he was old enough to select a tapestry for himself he preferred a piece with earth colors and land forms.

Kimry finished high school, visited with her Aunt Mim in Washington, D.C., for a while, and then went to Connecticut to the art school of the Norwich Free Academy that her father had attended.

Along with working at the Craft House, Kristina began another interesting project—teaching at the Taos Pueblo. She was asked if she would, under a Health, Education, Livelihood Program (HELP), assist in setting up a weaving cooperative at the Taos Pueblo, in the old granary building there. To begin, she had gone to the Pueblo Council meetings to explain and get permission for the project. The Council met almost every night to discuss Pueblo matters, and she went to several of these meetings while waiting her turn, in a candlelit room where the men sat in a circle, talking business in Tiwa. The meetings went on for hours, and it was midnight on the third evening before they finally got around to her topic on the agenda. She saw her role as getting the project started and then withdrawing, so she wanted to train an assistant who would eventually take over the directing of the cooperative. This was finally approved, and the Council hired a young Indian woman, Thelma Lujan, to work with her.

It was to be a co-op for selling not only weaving, but all crafts made at Taos Pueblo. These were primarily moccasins, beadwork, pottery, drums, some toys, and their beautiful traditional black, white, and red ceremonial belts. So they set up shop and began collecting equipment and materials. Kristina brought over several of her looms and the Indian School in Santa Fe loaned some also.

Women of all ages joined the group and took turns on the eight or so looms, working with the variety of wool yarn that Kristina ordered from her "mill-end" yarn sources. They wove rugs and shoulder bags to sell in the store. Women who knew the belt-weaving technique taught it to others, and to Kristina as well, and frames for weaving belts were made in the shop. Kristina loved working with these women as they enjoyed themselves thoroughly, "always laughing and carrying on as they worked."

Other people began to bring in things to sell—pottery, crocheting, dolls, ribbon shirts, and Navajo-style shirts. From work sold in the store a 10 percent commission was taken for the running of the shop. They bought rabbit skins and made moccasins with the fur inside, which were very popular, especially the ones made for babies, and fur-lined and beaded eyeglass cases. As the project grew more space was needed, and they built a room onto the original granary building to house the looms.

Then the co-op went into the rabbit-skin weaving business. Kristina read in Ruth Underhill's book, *Pueblo Crafts,* that rabbit-skins were used to weave blankets long before wool was available. In these blankets rabbit-skin strips were wrapped around a yucca-fiber cord when wet, so that they dried securely together; this became the blanket's warp, into which was worked, by a *twining* technique, the weft of yucca string, producing a blanket that was furry on both sides. They decided to try to make such a blanket on a regular loom and, after experimenting for a while, came up with a system that produced very similar-appearing rabbit-skin blankets. The Taos Pueblo weavers became quite well-known for these blankets and one was purchased by the Smithsonian. The Millicent Rogers Museum now also has one in its collection, and they are in other museums as well.

Anthropologists who saw the blankets pronounced them very similar in appearance to the early ones, though the method used for making them was quite different. The weavers and Kristina made an agreement that none of them would tell their method to anyone outside of the Pueblo, so it is still a secret. Two women still weave the blankets, one on her own loom at home and the other in Kristina's weaving studio, where there is a loom with the right warp ready.

After about a year, Kristina, as she says, "sort of faded out, which was the original plan," and Thelma Lujan continued to run the program until the building was torn down and replaced by a new one to house the Visitor's Center.

During that winter Oli went to New York where he had a show at the Stable Gallery and stayed on into the spring to find a studio. Before he returned for the summer, friends helped me move back across the valley once more, to El Salto, just above Arroyo Seco, a short stroll from the Craft House, and there Kimry joined us for the summer. Kristina had begun her Truchas weaving project, and now Rachel was developing and expanding the Craft House on her own.

A friend, Eya Fechin Branham (daughter of the Russian emigre artist Nicolai Fechin, who lived in Taos), asked Rachel to help her pick out a loom for her daughter from a group of them belonging to the University of New Mexico, which she had heard were stored up at the Lawrence Ranch north of Taos. (This was the large mountainside ranch that adjoined the Hawk Ranch where Dorothy Brett, many years before, had built her log cabin with the superb view off to the west; the popular story has been that D. H. and Frieda Lawrence became its owners by a trade to Mabel Dodge Luhan of the manuscript of his *Sons and Lovers*. Later the ranch passed to the University of New Mexico and was used, among other things, as a summer residence for working writers.) It was a very busy time for Rachel, and she kept putting off the expedition with Eya, but finally they set a day and drove up to the ranch. The caretaker took them out to a large storage building, and when he rolled open its big doors Rachel could hardly believe what she saw—seven gorgeous looms, some of them enormous.

She gasped and jokingly said, "I'll take that one—and that one . . ." and he answered, "Well, how much will you give me for those?"

Rachel protested, "Oh, I'm sorry. I don't have any money." But he persisted, "Seriously, how much would you give me for all of them?"

"Well, I suppose I could come up with two hundred dollars."

"Can you have them out of here by Saturday?"

She answered, "I certainly will," though at the moment she had no idea how, or how she would find the two hundred dollars, which at that point in her finances seemed like an immense sum. They picked out a loom for Eya's daughter and departed.

Somehow Rachel managed to raise the money and on the appointed day, she and Malcolm and Fred Fair drove up to the ranch in a flatbed truck, paid the two hundred dollars, and hauled all the looms away. And that was how she got the Craft House really going as a production weaving shop. Some of the looms needed some work, but the variety of weaving widths and types was very helpful for her. Two of them were old fly-shuttle looms that had been used somewhere in New Mexico for production weaving.

Rachel loaned me one of the new looms, six feet in width and, in my new home, I wove a large tapestry called *Brown Landscape*. A friend, Beth Rusnell, and I wove the plain opening section, throwing the shuttle between us across this broad loom. While I wove that last and largest New Mexico tapestry, the children—mine and those of neighbors on either side of us, the Grants and the Torres—kept an eye on Conor, playing out in the grove of trees and the pond that it surrounded, behind the house. Lorelei often spent the day, and after work Rachel would come up for a visit. Somehow the girls contrived to repair a small raft. One afternoon Jenny and Lorelei invited us to bring our drinks out to the pond where we found two chairs arranged on the raft for us, and they proudly poled us around the pond as the lowering sun illuminated the trees with the brightest green of the day.

The influx of "hippies" into the area in the mid-sixties proved to be a great benefit for Rachel and her Craft House. She began an apprentice program and put these young people to work at the new looms and taught them spinning as well. The managing of the Craft House, including all the work of bookkeeping and planning and teaching the apprentices proved to be very generative for her. She fixed up a small back room in the building and began having exhibits for other craftsmen. She had a show of Paul Soldner's work and one of Frances Graves's *colcha* embroidery. Cynthia Homire, a Santa Fe potter and friend, and I had a show of pottery and tapestries together.

Oli rented a studio in New York from an old painter friend, Clay Spohn, who had formerly lived in Taos, and came home and worked in a room of the Arroyo Seco school for the summer, planning to return to the city in the fall. I decided to move east also, and we arranged for me to live out in the little village of Remsenburg on Long Island for the winter in a house loaned to us by people who had collected both of our work. I didn't want to take Conor to live in the city, and Oli could escape to the country for weekends. Kimry was now working as a calligrapher for Hallmark Cards in Kansas City, after spending a year at the Minneapolis School of Art. So we made the move, and Jenny and Conor and I settled into a very different setting, a large old New England white clapboard house in the tree-filled village of Remsenburg.

Del Sol

After Kristina and Rachel's Craft House had been going on for almost two years, Kristina was finding it difficult to get much of her own work done along with shop-sitting; she was broke and discouraged as the winter slowly came to an end.

Then, late one night an acquaintance from Santa Fe called and asked, "How would you like to start a weaving business up in Truchas?" Without a moment's hesitation she said "Yes!" The friend explained that he worked for HELP (Health, Education, Livelihood Program), an anti-poverty program that was planning to set up various projects in economically depressed villages of northern New Mexico to create local employment. In Truchas the idea was to set up a weaving enterprise in which the weavers in the area could work at what they knew best, rather than have to find other kinds of work in order to survive. Many of these people had been weaving on a piece-work basis for the Ortega family weaving business in the nearby village of Chimayo. Fine traditional Spanish rugs and blankets had been woven there for generations, and the Ortegas employed many weavers to work for them in their own homes. However, it was thought that with an equipped shop and some marketing supervision their skills could benefit them more by working in their own shop. So this was Kristina's challenge—to set up and run a little village factory. It was an ideal one for her and, overnight, life became busy and exciting again. She arranged for Ian to spend a few weeks with old friends in Las Vegas and began driving daily the sixty miles over the mountains to Truchas as spring spread over the northern country.

A large building in the village was rented, and twelve weavers signed up for the project right away. They moved their looms into the shop and the space was arranged, ready for production as soon as the first shipments of yarn arrived. Kristina found a source in Ohio for good middle-weight single-ply wool yarn, dyed to her specifications. Using Putnam dyes she worked up a set of colors, making sample swatches in the soft range of vegetable-dyed colors, the kind she usually wove with herself. The plan was to produce rugs in simple stripes, both more contemporary and faster to weave than the traditional intricately patterned ones they were used to weaving. She wanted them to have a distinctive look of the Southwest, but also to appeal to the general market around the country.

Truchas had always been a place of mystery to us—beautiful, but strange and somewhat forbidding, even dangerous—a place where Anglos were not welcome. It was one of our favorite drives, especially at the changing of the seasons—east over the mountains from Ranchos de Taos, through the series of villages beginning with Penasco that were tucked in the high valleys, isolated by their location along the eastern edge of the mountains from the main north-south travel route that followed the Rio Grande. Each village had a distinctive quality in its setting and even in the look of its architecture. Las Trampas seemed open and sun-bathed, with houses of light golden-tan adobe. Then a little south of it was Truchas, higher yet. The village and surrounding fields spread over a wide level plateau in the midst of rising peaks; the main street ran along the very edge of this plain, from which you looked abruptly down into the valley below and out to the farther waves of mountains. The houses here were a darker earth color and most of them had steep-pitched tin roofs, indicating a heavier winter snowfall than our own valley. The highest of the peaks towering above is Truchas Peak to the southeast, with an altitude of 13,103 feet. It was one of the mountain presences in our daily lives in Taos also, high enough to be visible to us over the intervening mountains, where with North Truchas and Middle Truchas Peaks it forms a majestic complex—distant, serene, and with its north face toward Taos, showing white with the earliest snows of winter and keeping its snow longest in the spring.

Traveling into that country always seemed like going back in time and we knew that even the Spanish spoken there belonged to an earlier century. There was a legend of one of the long succession of priests who came from Spain to tend a parish in one of the New World mountain villages; after thirty years of studying and teaching the classics of the sixteenth century, he arrived and found, to his delight, the people of his parish speaking the Spanish of Cervantes.

Some years later Kristina and I spent two weeks wandering by car through Scotland and onto the Isle of Skye. On one of the remote fingers of Skye we found a village that reminded us startlingly of New Mexico, though at first we couldn't tell why. At the head of an inlet of the sea a fairly wide valley reached inland, crossed by long fields. Along the ridge above the valley on either side clustered the small stone cottages of the villagers, each looking out over their fields stretched below. On Skye, as in northern New Mexico, there is a special luminous quality to the air, and combined with the familiar arrangement of houses perched above the valley fields, the whole effect was strangely like a glimpse of home.

Truchas was first settled in 1754, a little more than sixty years after the great uprising of the Indians along the Rio Grande, when they had finally united to throw off the oppressive yoke of Spanish rule and either killed or driven out every Spanish settler and priest. In 1692 the Spanish had successfully returned to their capital in Santa Fe. Churches were reestablished in the Rio Grande pueblos, and an uneasy peace was taken up again. When the settlers in these back-mountain areas were granted their land, they were told to build their houses as a solid quadrangle surrounding a plaza with only one access large enough for the passage of one cart, so that they might have a stronghold in which to defend themselves should the Indians rise again. But those troubles did not come to their remote valley, and gradually the people spread out to form the traditional farming-village pattern, each family living at the head of the long strip of land granted it by the King of Spain. This disposition of property gave to each settler some of each sort of land, from the rich bottomland for farming in the valley to the drier land on the ridge where the houses were usually built, a pattern similar to that we saw in the valley on Skye.

Over the century since then, Truchas and the other villages back in the mountains had survived as quite separate cultural entities, preserving longest their traditional way of life, little diluted by the progress of the twentieth century along the Rio Grande. People departed rather than arrived. Children went off to college, men took employment in Española to the north of Santa Fe or in Los Alamos, seventy miles to the west. But generally things continued in the old patterns in the village.

Now, the old building on the main street beside the little river was alive with new activity. Kristina and the weavers were getting acquainted as they set in motion the new workshop. The first shipments of yarn arrived—vast quantities of it; soon shelves and baskets of colored yarns lined the walls. It was clear right away that these were skilled, experienced weavers. Most of them had woven for the shop in Chimayo for years; some of them were seventh-generation weavers in their families. They were of all ages, both men and women. Two of the best weavers were an older couple, the Cordovas, and there were also cousins, sisters, and sisters-in-law.

Kristina found herself learning a lot about production weaving from them, too. They put on great long warps with ease and they wove with amazing speed. Rugs came pouring off the looms, and she was at first hard put to keep ahead of them with designs. Most of the rugs were one-of-a-kind, partly because they hadn't each color in large enough quantities to do repeats and partly because it was more interesting that way and encouraged the exploring of variations. Kristina retired to her little office and worked out designs on graph paper, attaching swatches of yarn to the different stripes. Very quickly she learned to design good, simple stripes without pondering over them.

These were all stand-up looms. The weaver stood on the two treadles and, by shifting weight from one foot to the other, opened first one shed and then the alternate one. Kristina was amazed at how tightly each weaver strung the warps, expecting the old looms to fly apart, but this tautness produced a good wide-open shed to fling the shuttle through. Weaving in this standing position was much less tiring since it was never necessary to lean over the weaving as one does when sitting at a loom. The body is constantly in motion, moving from side to side but always in a balanced posture. She watched with fascination the fancy footwork patterns and the flourish of throwing the shuttle, the whole like a Weavers' Dance. The looms were old, all handmade by some past generation in the family. When something wore out or broke, a new part was made, so each loom was of many ages, but the original machine was in some cases the work of someone many generations back.

The feeling in the shop was warm and friendly, and there seemed to be no prejudice against Kristina as an outsider. It was as though they, being isolated in this tiny village, had not been around enough Anglos to develop the bias she sometimes felt around Taos. She felt that she was part of a large, jolly, hard-working family. Not only had she, through the project, escaped from a low point in her own working career, but the weavers also enjoyed this new work setting. Instead of weaving alone at home in bits of time between the never-ending household activities, they were working full time at their craft and doing it with other professionals, a change that was both stimulating and fun. When a rug was finished and cut from the loom it was spread out on the big work table and looked at by everyone. A sales area was set up and customers began coming into the shop; it was exciting to the weavers to see people buy their work, people who usually wanted to meet the person who had woven it. Everyone took part, also, in the discussions about variations of designs or whether a design should be repeated.

Kristina was supremely happy with the whole thing. It seemed a perfect blending of energies and abilities—her love for working with people and solving organizational and production problems, the thoroughly professional weavers working at their top skills and also earning a better salary than they ever had before. All these factors made the feeling of energy and accomplishment high.

Rugs were piling up, and Kristina found a rather unconventional means of making their first introduction to the outside marketplace. She got the name of the head of Design Research, a good store in Boston with branches around the country, packed up a huge box of rugs, and sent it off to him without advance warning, sure that if he actually saw them, the rugs would sell themselves. She was right—within a matter of days he called, saying, "I'm flying out!" and a few days later he was at their doorstep. Together, they designed a whole line of products for his stores—mostly rugs, but also pillows and stoles. He wanted even simpler designs in the rugs than they had been making and though quite elegant, they weren't quite as interesting to produce. The venture was wildly successful, though, and hundreds of rugs sold.

This sudden success produced some disadvantages, too. At first the office in Albuquerque had left them completely to their own devices. This independence was good in many ways, though there were small annoyances such as lost vouchers for yarn orders that caused delays in getting materials. Now, with the sudden and monumental increase in sales and orders, they became the focus of much more attention from Albuquerque. The home office now became interested in all details of the Truchas shop and, naturally, this complicated the daily planning and functioning of the operation. Success had created its problems.

Of course, they were now using great quantities of yarn. Various changes were made in the workings and arrangement of the workroom. As Kristina watched the stripes grow under the weavers' hands she realized that some of them were giving a second beat to each thread as a sort of rhythmic emphasis; she finally convinced them that over a day's time they were making thousands of beats that weren't necessary, and they altered their patterns of weaving motion to correct the wasted effort.

The senior weaver in the shop was Alfredo Cordova, whose wife was also one of the weavers. He had a tiny boat shuttle that he had woven with all his life. Kristina had found somewhere a huge shuttle that held at least twice as much yarn as his. As she watched him work she calculated that if he would use her larger shuttle, a rug that now took him about eight hours to weave would probably take about two hours less, because of the time saved in filling bobbins. But he was a stubborn man and firmly refused to give up the old shuttle. Finally she begged him, "Just today, use it." And he gave in. Sure enough, he made the rug in six hours and he was bursting with pride. He flung the rug out on the table with a grand gesture and refused ever to give up that shuttle again, so Kristina found a carpenter to make more of them.

As orders increased, various other efficient shortcuts were worked out. One person began doing all the bobbin winding so that each weaver had a supply of colors ready at hand. The organization of the shop was becoming as effective as the weaving was skilled and Kristina loved all of it. She seems to have two strong currents of talent in her makeup—a fascination with organization and an equally strong artistic bent—both of which are easy to see in relation to parental influence from her father, a New

England manufacturer, and her mother, a painter. Her strong
humanist leaning is harder to link, unless it comes from her ma-
ternal grandfather, William McDougall, who came to this country
from England to do pioneering work in extrasensory perception
at Duke University in North Carolina. At any rate, all of her
talents were getting good exercise at Del Sol Weavers.

Everyone gathered around the big work table for lunch and
talk. One day Kristina asked the staff if they liked working at the
shop or if they would rather be weaving at home. Everyone
assured her they would much rather come to work, saying that
if they were home they'd be busy canning and butchering and
taking care of everything. It was almost like rest for them. They
loved it. Still, after an eight-hour day at their looms they often
went home and put up bushels of chiles or canned a few dozen
quarts of fruit. They were usually ahead of time for work and
Kristina gave them keys to let themselves in in the morning. They
meticulously took only ten-minute breaks and never more than
a half-hour for lunch. With impeccable integrity they shared the
responsibility for the smooth running of the enterprise and its
increasing success. When summer came the Cordovas loaned
Kristina and Ian a little cabin so they wouldn't have to make the
daily drive from Taos.

Then another aid to production appeared. One of the weavers
showed Kristina an old machine that was stored up in the attic
of his house—a big warp-winding wheel like nothing she had
ever seen before. It was fifteen feet in circumference, and on it
warps of great length could be wound very rapidly, with all of
the warp ends ready to be transferred to the warp beam of the
loom. They decided they needed one in the shop, and Kristina
asked one of the weavers to build it. He then became the warp-
maker for all the looms and became an expert, usually putting
on eighty-foot warps. It was a great help with the continuing
increase in orders.

Toward the end of the summer Kristina and a man from the
state office made a trip to New York, primarily to visit the Ford
Foundation, which was providing much of their funding. Kristina's stepmother lived there at the time and, pronouncing her
stepdaughter's Taos clothes unsuitable, dressed her up properly
for tea at the Ford Foundation. They also visited the wholesale
showrooms in the vast Gift Building and there made what turned

out to be a most valuable contact. While wandering around the showroom they stopped to talk to two sisters who had a permanent showroom for work from India. These women were particularly interested in the Truchas project because they had developed a similar one in a village in India. The people there had traditionally made beautiful laquerware, but the village was in a poverty-stricken state when they first arrived. The sisters got involved, designing things for the villagers to make that would be salable in the United States and then marketed the work for them; the result was that now the village was thriving and self-sufficient. They decided to give Del Sol Weavers a portion of their New York showroom, and thus another market was established.

This turn of events produced great excitement back in the mountains. The success was gratifying, but the serene productivity was somewhat altered. Now, visits from officials of the Albuquerque office were more frequent, and there seemed to be a growing difference in point of view in relation to the project. One of these visits was particularly disturbing. A man from the home office arrived one day and looked over the operation, then pulled out a stopwatch and—positioning himself beside one of the older and most experienced weavers—began to time him at his work. The dignified older gentleman continued working, but turned white as a ghost, and Kristina could see that he was terribly insulted, trembling in silent rage. Nor was this a necessary gesture; Kristina knew exactly how long it took to weave an inch— or an entire rug—as did the weavers themselves. Later there was even an effort to put in time clocks and to take away the keys that she had given the weavers to let themselves in to work early, but Kristina was fortunately able to halt these efforts.

The project became the focus of a lot of attention. Alex Mercure, head of HELP for the state, came up and talked with Kristina about his plans for expanding the project with fifteen shops sprinkled over northern New Mexico, setting each of them up on the pattern of Del Sol Weavers. He and Kristina went on the radio in Taos to talk about it all. Visiting dignitaries appeared from Washington and other places to look over the "model project." Kristina was to particularly remember one woman who took her aside and praised the accomplishment, saying, "This is a fabulous project, but it will never work because it's run by a bureaucracy."

Again Kristina and the Albuquerque representative went on

a trip out into the world, this time to the big Gift Show in Los Angeles. They took a showroom, and orders for these southwestern rugs poured in from wholesale buyers—thousands of them. Suddenly they were selling rugs so fast they could hardly keep up. Also, they were given a salesman on the road.

At the beginning of the second summer the Cordovas' son, Harry, who had just graduated from business school, applied for a summer job. Kristina called the Albuquerque office and was told that she couldn't hire him—that it would be nepotism. She persisted and finally got permission to do so on a temporary basis. He worked out very well. His bookkeeping skills relieved Kristina of some of that kind of work, and gradually his role developed into that of office manager. The addition of Harry to the staff also helped to make possible the next development.

The building in Truchas was becoming crowded, and the great quantity of shipping was getting awkward from the small post office there, but they arrived at a perfect solution to these combined problems. The Thorne House, a lovely old building on one of the main streets in Taos, was standing empty, and Kristina arranged to rent it, moving all of the finishing work and the shipping there. Harry was able by this time to take over the running of the weaving part of the business in Truchas, with Kristina coming over the mountain only two days a week.

This worked out splendidly. Thorne House was large, and there was also space for a showroom and retail outlet. They moved in a couple of looms and hired people from the Taos area to do the finishing work—knotting the fringes of rugs and making pillows and bags—and some weaving as well. It was an amazing success; retail sales were tremendous, and soon the Thorne House outlet was making a great difference in the financial picture of the project as a whole. Selling retail—direct to the customers without the middleman—was so much more profitable that the proceeds paid everyone's salary as well as the rents for both buildings. Also it meant that Kristina could live at home and spend much less time traveling and could put Ian back in the local school.

One of the prices paid for success was the necessity to standardize their products. No longer were the rug designs constantly changing, a loss particularly to the weavers. Now they put out a brochure showing available designs and wove those to fill orders. Only at the Taos shop could one-of-a-kind things be sold.

In a way, the Taos shop took on the more creative character that the Truchas workshop had in the beginning.

Friction mounted with the increased interaction between the project and the home office. One source was the question of profit-sharing. In the begining of the project the weavers had been told that as soon as the business started making a profit, they would share in it. When business grew by such phenomenal strides, Kristina periodically asked the office about this but was always told, "Oh, no, you're still losing money." From her own bookkeeping she felt sure that they had to be making a profit. The unavoidable conclusion to be drawn was that the profit from Del Sol Weavers was being absorbed by the other Del Sol projects that hadn't yet seen the same success. Kristina made only about four dollars an hour for her work in developing and running the project. This hadn't particularly bothered her as she was managing and she absolutely loved her job, though it was more than full time with the commuting and overseeing both parts of the enterprise, and it used all her energy. But business continued to thrive. New people were employed in Taos, and that outlet continued to bring in a lot of customers. Del Sol was approaching its second anniversary.

Small frictions over the running of the project continued and finally Kristina decided that her work with it was done and she resigned. The project continued without her for about six months and then finally closed down.

After a while the Cordova family opened their own weaving shop which is still functioning—very successfully—with just Mr. and Mrs. Cordova and their son, Harry, who manages the shop and has also become a fine weaver. They do a thriving business, barely keeping up with the demand for their work. Kristina asked them why they didn't hire some of their relatives, but they said that they like it just the way it is. "We don't want to get any bigger; it's just fine."

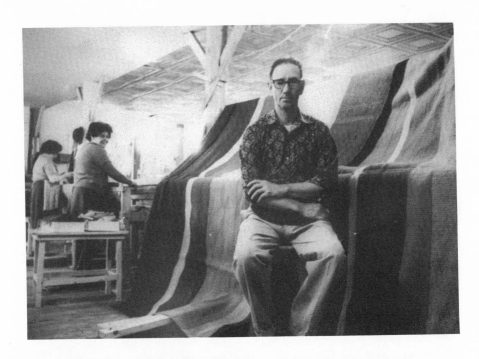

ABOVE: *Alfredo R. Cordova with a large completed rug in the Truchas workshop of the Del Sol project.*
LEFT: *Harry Cordova weaving a rug.*

Mrs. Cordova and her sister in the workshop.

LEFT: *Weighing up a batch of yarn.*
BOTTOM: *A lunchtime planning meeting.*

Back East

Through our first fall back East, while Jenny was in school, Conor and I spent our days exploring the uncrowded winter beaches and the interesting terrain of country Long Island, a very peaceful interlude. It was, for Oli and me, an unplanned but nevertheless real trial separation and a parting of the ways, and from that time on he spent his winters in his studio in the city.

I was invited by Jack Larsen to take part in the tapestry show that he was planning for 1968 at the Museum of Modern Art. I was not weaving and was much involved in my quiet year with Conor and Jenny and did not take part in the show. But through Jack I met a weaver, Thelma Becherer, who lived in a nearby village and became a fast friend for all three of us. She and Conor and I took picnics to sheltered, sunny spots along the shore and, bundled up, watched the half-frozen surf turn to a turgid, rolling mass of gray along the beaches. I had, years before, spent a winter above a Cape Cod beach, and this was for me a sort of return to a particular kind of winter experience, a quiet time that I needed. I had no urge to be weaving tapestries. I had always worked at them when there was a *need* to, when there was something that I needed to explore through them. It seemed that I needed a break; to weave now would be like turning out pretty watercolors, things that had no real reason for being; so I didn't.

Oli often came out on the train for weekends, and occasionally friends from the city escaped for visits with us. Then in the spring we gave our house back to its owners and all went to Wellfleet, Massachusetts, on the Cape for the summer—familiar terrain, though we hadn't been there since Jenny's first summer, after which we made our first Return to Taos. So some kind of circle was now complete.

The Eriksons were at their cottage in Cotuit and we visited

them. Just inside their door hung the now rather primitive looking *Sunflowers* tapestry that Joan had provoked me to make for her years before in Taos, and in Erik's study hung a painting of Oli's. Joan told me about the Activities Program she was involved in, had in fact originated, at the Austen Riggs Center, a small private psychiatric hospital and research center in Stockbridge, Massachusetts, and planted the idea that I might want to get busy again soon and come to teach weaving there. Rachel and the children came east to visit her parents in New Hampshire during the summer and visited us on the Cape, so I got a firsthand report of weaving activities in New Mexico. The Craft House was thriving; she now had eight people working for her, weaving and spinning, and she showed us slides of the tapestries she had woven over the past year. She was showing her work in area exhibits in New Mexico, Colorado, and Arizona and also had been asked to jury several shows. She loved working at her full capacity, organizing and expanding the Craft House facilities to their greatest potential. Now, running the shop on a consignment basis, she showed the work of 120 New Mexico craftpeople. At that time there were only a few craft shops in New Mexico—Artesanos in Las Vegas, Alice Parrot's shop in Santa Fe, and the Hootens's shop in Old Town Albuquerque. She reported that Kristina's Del Sol project in Truchas and Taos was going well. This period, which was such a quiet one for me, was for both of them one of expanding and experimentation.

Through Thelma Becherer, I had rented a house in East Quogue to return to in the fall, where Jenny could continue in the same school. It was a small wood and glass house set on an unpaved sandy street in the midst of low oak and pine woods, very different from the New England village setting of Remsenburg. Conor, now three, loved it and took up tree climbing, and on our sorties to the beaches we began collecting driftwood and beach lumber to bring home for building a treehouse. The house grew through the fall between two small twisting oak trunks. It was a grand project that tied the winter together—piled high with snow and unusable for several months, then repaired and expanded upward into the trees' intertwining branches in the early spring when we again could range the beaches for building materials. Conor liked the idea that these were *imported* materials— had arrived here from far-flung points.

Another favorite haunt was an extensive wildlife refuge with trails wandering around lowland ponds and swamps and a small wild zoo where he became acquainted with talking crows and exotic birds. There also was a large flock of wild turkeys and some spotty-feathered guinea fowl, and we collected their feathers and took them home. A bit of the weaving urge was returning, and I set up a Navajo loom and wove a strange wool and feather tapestry. That fall I had a small tapestry show in an Easthampton gallery of pieces woven in New Mexico.

Then in the spring I went up to visit the Riggs Activities Department in Stockbridge and brought along some tapestries for a small exhibit. The education program of the hospital was housed in a separate building in the middle of the town, in appearance and function a small arts school where patients from the center participated as students in workshops in jewelry, woodworking, photography, pottery, painting, and also in a theatre group. In other buildings were a working greenhouse and a nursery school in which patients were assistant teachers. There had been, in former years, a weaving workship of the usual institutional kind with row upon row of looms, where patients wove during the day and instructors re-wove after hours. More recently weaving had been for a time revived with a contemporary weaving instructor. For some years, however, the looms had simply been stored away. The director of this Activities Program was David Loveless, who, over the years he had been there, had taught the pottery, jewelry, woodworking, and photography workshops.

I was invited to start up the weaving workshop again and was intrigued with the idea, so at the beginning of the summer we made the move to Stockbridge. We found a small house surrounded by tall trees and woods, on a quiet street near the shop and—with Conor happily enrolled in the nursery school—I went to work.

We set up one loom, but it was not the center of activity. From the beginning I focused the work in the weaving room on process rather than on products. My job was to involve these (mostly young) people in working, and it seemed to me that what would most enrich their lives and occupy their working time creatively was to simply become involved in studying textile materials and discovering interesting ways to use them. So I accumulated yarns of all sorts—string, beautiful colored wools—

any kind of fiber that I came upon—and we *played around with them*. We knotted and crocheted and knitted; we made small frames and invented ways of weaving on them; we made belt looms of the most basic sort.

Participation in activities at the shop was completely voluntary. Some of the students had become very skilled in one area or another, and individual work went on alongside tentative beginnings by newcomers, who were sometimes simply exploring this new setting where people, both students and teachers, were obviously *involved* with something intriguing. There was a shop coffee pot and a small area in the front of the workshop where work by students and teachers was for sale to the public, and the social atmosphere was informal and inviting.

As my students became more interested or skilled in a particular area or technique, we invented ways or equipment needed to carry out projects that they wanted to work on. The main thing, though, was that they *acquired interest in and familiarity with* materials; the materials became their allies in developing skills in working. *Their interest and skill grew together.* Some of these students needed simply to spend time being absorbed in something, and for some it was very gratifying to acquire sufficient skill to make things that were bought by visitors to the shop store. Others became interested in weaving as a craft or discipline and wanted to study intensely and become professional weavers. I loved working on these different levels and enjoyed the challenge of finding ways of making the process of working with fibers intriguing, of helping people learn to enjoy studying and exploring on their own.

A New Life

The work in the shop was very involving, and I did little weaving myself during those years. Kimry moved east from Kansas City to join us, and when we moved to an apartment that included studio space she decided to open a craft shop there, which she called The Craft House. She had begun to do very fine beadwork, took the work of other craftpeople on consignment, then set up a loom and began weaving pillows for the shop. Oli and I were divorced in 1973.

Though a number of the doctors at Riggs, therapists of the patients, our students, also worked on projects in the shop, it seemed that it would be beneficial for the medical staff in general to become more familiar with what actually went on there for their patients, and David Loveless and I planned a project to accomplish this. We taped interviews with a variety of patients for whom different areas of the program had become particularly important, and I wrote these up for a presentation to the medical staff. We then decided that the entire Activities Program, which Joan Erikson had conceived and begun years before—and had brought David east from California to implement—should be recorded in some way. We talked it over with Joan and decided to write a book.

We taped more student–patient interviews, then we and Joan visited other psychiatric hospitals with what were usually called occupational therapy programs and expanded the concept to more correctly also include Activities Programs other than therapeutic ones in hospitals, especially community activity programs. We received assistance from grants to work on the book from the Commonwealth Fund and the Grant Foundation, and David and I left Riggs to complete the project. The result was *Activity, Recovery, Growth, The Communal Role of Planned Activities*, with Joan

Erikson, which was published two years later, in 1975, just after David and I were married.

While still teaching at Riggs, my household had been joined by Jane Orr, a young music student, who had been Conor's teacher and then friend, and who took care of him when I was teaching. Then I finally achieved an ambition of long standing—buying a house—and we all moved into the country. Jenny went away for her third year of high school to High Mowing School in New Hampshire, Kimry eventually got her own apartment, Jane went away to college, and David and I bought a large old hardware store building in the nearby village of Housatonic.

But before starting the remodeling of that building for our workshop needs, we and Conor and Jenny made a trip to New Mexico—David's first and Conor's first Return; he was six. Emerging from the canyon, we stopped at Rini Templeton's home and studio on the brink of the valley, and she invited us to pitch our tent there. Rini was an old friend of mine and a newer one of David's; she had visited me in Stockbridge and taught a sculpture workshop for a few weeks at Riggs. That first night we were serenaded by coyotes, and the next day Conor saw his first "child of the earth," an alarming though harmless large insect of the cricket family, which had crawled into his shirt during the night. It was a perfect spot from which to visually introduce to David this valley that I had told him so much about, and we set off eagerly to find friends and explore in detail.

Rachel and Malcolm were divorced in 1969. After selling the Craft House in 1971, she went on an extended trip to South America. She had signed a contract with Alfred A. Knopf to write a weaving book, and during the next few years that would be her main focus of work. The book, which would be called *The Weaving, Spinning and Dyeing Book,* was an ambitious project, to be profusely illustrated with her line drawings and including weaving projects—blankets, rugs, and garments—of her own design.

Lorelei, Kinlock, and Seth were living in Ranchos as part of a group of young silversmiths in the rambling adobe home of an old friend, Sammy Heaton, whose children were also jewelers. Sammy's own work was fascinating—metal pictures with engraving, metal mosaic, and fired-on precious metals. She had created an atmosphere of disciplined and productive informality for these young people, and Jenny was, of course, intrigued. When we arrived we found everyone involved in a building project, adding a room to the adobe compound. They had almost reached the top of a wall and Conor was most impressed to see great quantities of mud being mixed, adobe bricks tossed to the workers up on the wall, and buckets of mud hauled up by rope.

We visited old friends of mine and spent time with Kristina in Arroyo Seco, where she had begun the process of adding to her little house. The tapestry-weaving students of her Taos Valley Weaving School were just finishing up the work on their looms in the weaving room she had built near her house and in the yard outside it. Her year now had taken on a new pattern, her time divided between teaching her weaving students in the summer and the beginning of a period of house-building with her friend Sandy Seth.

Jenny stayed with her friends in Ranchos while David, Conor, and I took off on an exploration of the country west of the Rio Grande, camping at night wherever we found ourselves and setting our route by a pamphlet we had found of mineral deposits in the area. It was a wonderful way to be led into the back country, and we often got permission to wander beyond ranch gates. We camped on an old Indian site beneath weathered cliffs still bearing the blackened smoke-stains of ancient campfires and found red pottery shards. Our old Volvo managed the rough terrain very well, though we occasionally had to get out and reconstruct bits of road over washes. Conor loved the country and added a lot to his already rich sense of natural history. We collected rocks and tucked them into all of the concavities of our vehicle, then reached our outer goal—Pueblo Bonito in Chaco Canyon—very beautiful and because it was late in the season with very few people around. Stone later became Conor's favorite building material, and it may be that seeing the masterful work with it at Bonito was the origin of his later sense of how to put stones together well.

It was hard to leave the valley, but we had to get back to work and Conor to school. Jenny had decided not to return for her last year at High Mowing and wanted very much to stay in Taos and learn silversmithing. We looked at a boarding school north of Taos for her, but decided against it, and convinced her to return east with us at least temporarily. Her interest was as strong as ever when we got home, though, and knowing that the Heaton household was well supervised by Sammy, we finally decided to let her return to board and study silversmithing for a while.

Back in Housatonic, we unloaded all of our mineral treasures at the old hardware store and set to the work of transforming it into a workshop-showroom. A young couple, Rosemary and Gordon Peery, both friends of Jenny's from High Mowing, had earlier visited us to ask if we had any interesting work projects that they could get involved in, and we had promised to let them know should something come up. This was a perfect project for the help of young eager hands, and they arrived and threw themselves wholeheartedly into the formidable project. We had to clear out the hardware store as well as the accumulation of decades of mostly useful debris and out-of-date merchandise that filled the storerooms behind it and an old carriage house at the back of the property. It was also necessary to remove from the vast upstairs room that ran the length and width of the building dozens of old television sets, trade-ins left over from the former proprietor's repair business.

We conducted a mammoth sale of the store merchandise and quantities of other things we thought we wouldn't need, Conor happily in charge of the candy counter and Rosemary, the old cash register. An actual crowd was waiting outside when we opened the doors, and we rid ourselves of a great mass of goods, but it was only the beginning of clearing space for the plans we had. After separating out the useful objects, David and Gordon took ten truckoads of old television sets, old but unappealing display stands, cans of withered paint, and other junk to the dump, and we began the process of reflooring, putting up walls, installing bathrooms, until finally we had created a small apartment for Rosemary and Gordon to move into and a space for a larger one for us when more urgent work was done. While putting in the plumbing they discovered the trolley tracks, which we had been told by the former owner had been used to strengthen the second story when the building was rebuilt after a fire. In the old days, he said, the trolley ran down all the way from Vermont, stopping just across the street. The store, then three stories, had twenty employees, and the second floor had been the furniture department. That was when the large textile mill buildings that now stood empty along the river flowing through the town were in full production, weaving bedspreads on great Jaquard looms. In exploring those buildings, we had found stacks of gray cardboard loom-programmers, cards with holes in them in patterns that created the various weaves. We hung some of these in the store for area dividers and backgrounds.

Rosemary and Gordon deserved the grandest of domiciles for the incredibly hard work they had done, but seemed quite content with this high-ceilinged and hastily constructed home, furnished with odds and ends that we unearthed on the premises and with their pet, Bad Cat, happily settled in. We, too, were eager to live at the store as soon as we could. Our general aim, as much as possible, was to make our life all of a piece—to blend our work and our play simply as different tenses of the same experience.

The transformation of the store downstairs into a spacious workshop-showroom was dramatic. The walls, when they turned from apple-green to white, set off the floor-to-ceiling varnished shelves beautifully and we set up my looms and spinning wheel at one end of the room and filled the shelves with yarn and, gradually, with weaving.

Through the spring and summer we continued the remodeling of the labyrinth of storage areas into usable space, finally including the construction of a second apartment. Dirty and exhausted, we would, to Conor's delight, lock up and all take lunch to the river and swim, eat, and nap until we were revived, then return to our labors. Gradually we could take more and more time for doing new work rather than creating the setting for it. David and Gordon cleared the old shop behind the store and moved David's woodworking tools into it, and he got to work, first making things needed for furnishing the store, then beginning to make things to sell in it—wood turnings and lovely simple chestnut and oak dining tables. Along with this, he resumed the house designing he had done along with teaching through the years. And I began weaving tapestries again.

It was a wonderful space in which to work. Traffic through the village of Housatonic was light, but most of our customers returned and sent their friends. With the addition of people who had known David's work over the years, there seemed to be a rather ideal flow—enough but not so much that we couldn't concentrate on our work. At the front of the store were large show windows; we filled these with work and they served as our sole advertising. Later, when we finished and moved into our apartment upstairs, we left lights on in the show windows at night and would often hear a screech of brakes late in the evening when passersby stopped to inspect the contents of the windows. Then the next day they would return to see the rest of the shop.

When the major work of reconstruction was done, Rosemary and Gordon and Bat Cat returned to New Hampshire and other activities—Rosemary to work for a landscaper and Gordon to work for a while in a restaurant. No greater good fortune could be wished for by anyone undertaking a monstrous new enterprise than to have a pair like this come along and ask, "Are you doing anything interesting that we could help you with?"

On our days off, we and Conor would gather our two dogs, some food and fishing poles, a book and writing materials for me, and, choosing a direction we hadn't gone in recently, take off on an exploring expedition. This gradually evolved into something of an art, selecting roads that would lead to something rewarding—rivers with fish, quarries with intriguing stone to take home with us, fruit to can or nuts to store, plants to set in pots in the store, flowers to be gathered. And we discovered river walking—taking off in shorts and old sneakers up or downstream in some unfamiliar small river, delighted to find an artery for viewing the countryside other than roads, and one that was never posted. When we came to a deep spot we went for a swim; David and Conor became adept at catching fish with their hands and catching crayfish, which I collected in a plastic bag until we had enough to take home for a small feast.

From these expeditions we furnished the store with interesting objects, plants, collections of stones, which added little to our inventory but much to the general atmosphere, and people enjoyed the variety of things to be looked at. It was a wonderful luxury to have enough space to surround ourselves with any materials that intrigued us, some of which we might use someday to make something. One of the legacies from the hardware store was a wide, twelve-foot-long counter with two rows of bins underneath that had held nails of different sorts and sizes. This became my work table and I filled the bins with unspun wool in many colors. Since much of our walls were covered still with shelves, David constructed a hanging section of wall for a large tapestry that I wove and when someone wanted to buy it as well as the tapestry, he simply made another one.

This was the beginning of the fuel crisis, and David designed an iron and brick fireplace that he had produced in a foundry and sold in the store. He found a source for soft, rosy-colored old brick and made low iron tables in which to combine brick and a planter tray, which we filled with rocks we collected and different kinds of succulents. We heated our apartment with a fine ornate old woodstove that had been retired for years in the recesses of a storage room. It was quite a curiosity to Conor's friends who had never seen such a thing; though in a few years, of course, they became commonplace.

Above David's wood shop was an unfinished storage area which we finally incorporated into living space. Jenny came home for a visit and we made it into an apartment for her, hoping that she would stay and set up her own jewelry workshop. When the old floor was uncovered and finally sanded, it was found to be made of a dozen different kinds of wood—chestnut, maple, several kinds of oak, cherry, ash, beech, pine, fir, and birch.

She potted ferns brought home from the woods and made the tiny apartment very cozy. Then she set up a sewing area in the shop and made clothes to sell in the store, but after six months New Mexico drew her back. It seemed that silversmithing would likely become her chosen career, and back in Taos she would work in a cooperatively owned workshop with Lorelei, Seth, Kinlock, and other friends.

The last area to be renovated was a long, narrow room beyond my weaving area—the former TV repair shop. David and our friend Randy Wagner stripped linoleum from the floor and sanded it, stripped the wallboard from the outer wall to expose a dramatic rough stone wall, and plastered the opposite one with a quiet light gray, creating a fine gallery space. We inaugurated it with a show of David's wood turnings, my tapestries, and Randy's colorful paintings. Later, Rini Templeton came again from Taos for a visit, and we had a show of her sculptures.

The village of Housatonic clustered along both sides of the Housatonic River and beyond it the land rose to low mountains, to which I looked as I wove at my loom. On our side the town climbed less steeply to the woods of Pixley Hill. The building was tucked into this hill so that the second floor had an entrance at ground level in back with a little yard between it and the basement of the carriage house, which stepped up yet again to achieve another ground-level entrance on the uphill side. What we gradually made into our yard had once been the dooryard where wagonloads of coal for sale were deposited in the basement of the carriage house, an important business in those days. David and Conor cleared out the basement and went in search of a flock of chickens to live there. We were surprised that the only comment from our neighbors was that they enjoyed hearing the sound of a rooster again in the early morning. That first winter was a cold one, and one very frigid night they transported them to the basement of the store for the duration of the cold spell, just under where my loom stood, from where I, and occasionally surprised visitors, heard them clucking contentedly.

Then with the return of warm weather and the fishing season David and Conor found another use for the basement. They set up a twelve-foot plastic swimming pool on the dirt floor there, where a small window would give a bit of sunlight for part of the day; they filled the pool with water and, as the summer progressed, gradually filled it with trout and perch, intending it to be a fresh food source. The fish thrived and grew but were never eaten, and a year or so later were returned to the wilds of the Williams River.

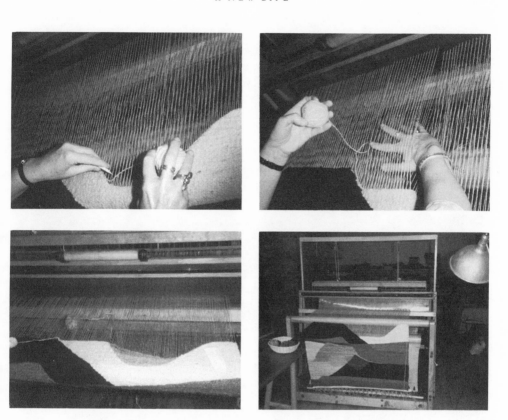

Joan building the shapes of a tapestry. Then, the weaving dropped down for study.

TOP: Horizontal in Golds and Naturals *(collection of Joan and Erik Erikson) hanging in Joan and David's Housatonic shop, with David's chestnut and iron dining table and candelabra.*
LEFT: Landscape in Naturals *(1974) with David's iron and brick table.*

Kristina's Projects

Kristina's next teaching project, in 1970, gave her a chance to carry out an idea she had had for years. A friend who worked in the state offices in Santa Fe as a nurse came by her house to visit one afternoon and asked her if she had any ideas for doing something with the disabled in the Taos area. When Kristina was working on the Truchas project she had passed, every day, a man—"a big, healthy fellow just sitting in a wheelchair out on his front portal"—and kept thinking, "Why can't we extend Del Sol to get some of these handicapped people working for us?" So she suggested this idea of teaching them to weave so they could be doing something interesting with their time as well as making some money. Her friend said she had money for a grant for the developmentally disabled and would see what she could do. This would be a part-time project, and Kristina could continue with her own work.

Back in Santa Fe, her friend got together funds for a very small grant for Kristina to work with eight disabled people. The first thing was to acquire looms—small ones that could be worked with more easily. She collected the looms, some on trips into Colorado and Arizona, then located the people in the area around Arroyo Seco and Taos.

She usually set up the looms for people, and most of them also had to be sat with as they worked; they were either retarded or physically handicapped or both. Some of them eventually were able to work on their own. One of the most successful was a man, paralyzed on one side of his body, who had learned to weave many years ago in a WPA program but hadn't done anything since because he had no money for a loom or materials.

He quickly got thoroughly involved. He and his mother lived together, and she would keep a supply of bobbins wound for him. At first Kristina provided him with designs from which he made narrow sixteen-inch weavings that he could manage with one hand. When she taught him the tapestry technique so that he could weave patterns other than stripes, he quickly got the idea and started weaving his own designs. He enjoyed it immensely and became very productive, selling the pieces as he wove them, first to friends, and then when he had a surplus, at the Los Alamos craft fair.

Another man who had learned to weave long ago, the father of nine or ten children, became very productive when provided with a loom and has been weaving ever since. Kristina saw him recently, now in his seventies, and he said, "I don't even have to try to sell. People just come here to buy them." He weaves rugs in wool and acrylic or whatever comes to hand in the traditional Chimayo style and had a piece in the recent exhibit of Hispanic crafts at the Taos Art Association gallery in Taos that Kristina curated.

Then there was a young retarded girl in Taos who made beautiful rag rugs. She lived alone with her father and he got involved too, the two of them competing for the loom. It brought excitement into their lives and she sold a number of rugs.

In one family of adult retarded sisters a woman who was unable to talk had six-year-old twin children who were very bright and caught on to the weaving the first day the loom was set up. They would stand, one on each side of her, and direct her: "Hey, Mom, it's time to change your foot."

After a year and a half the grant money ran out, but Kristina continued for a while longer because she enjoyed the people so much. Then an educational center for the adult retarded was set up in Taos and most of the looms were moved there, where the weavers could go to spend the day and work. She still runs into her students occasionally, and they invite her to come over and help them warp up looms again. Getting involved in getting people involved in weaving seems to be irresistible to her, and she drops in to see what they are doing; she remembers them as the most "joyful" students she has ever taught.

During this same period a project of another sort began to occupy her time. When she and Bucky Wilson, Ian's father, were first married they lived in Albuquerque and her old friend, Marina Mirabal, from Taos Pueblo, had come down to build a fireplace in their new home. Later, back in Taos, she worked with Marina to learn to construct these beautiful, simple traditional Indian corner fireplaces and with Marina's help, built several in her house as it continued to grow.

A friend, Sandy Seth, asked her to make one for her. Then together they built one for another friend, and this grew into an unplanned small business. Their first job was to build three fireplaces in one house, one of them a complicated affair with two openings. The older adobe houses often have several roofs built one on top of another; this one had four, and going through the roof with the chimney was quite a challenge. After a while Kristina stopped to get back to weaving, but Sandy loved the work and continued, building or supervising the construction of over a hundred of them around the valley.

Then one day Sandy called her with a new idea. "There's a little empty house down here in Lyman. Wouldn't it be fun to buy it and fix it up?" They dickered with the owner but couldn't come to an agreement. The idea was planted, though, and they became bolder and decided that maybe they should just start from scratch and build a house. Kristina had some savings, and they bought a piece of land from a friend and did just that. Both of them had built additions to their own houses, but this was rather a daring project, planning and building on their own a new house to sell.

It turned out to be a great partnership. They saw eye to eye and managed to work together at designing as they went, without drawing up plans on paper. Kristina recalls that often one of them would say something like, "What do you think of . . ." and the other would finish the sentence. "It grew—it wasn't all on paper— we invented as we went." They were both very fond of traditional adobe houses, and in this house they included adobe, wood, and tile detailing that made it quite unique for new construction— *trasteros,* or cabinets, built into walls, handmade doors inspired by the cut-out crosses in old graveyards that Kristina was so fond of. At that time, before the revival of traditional adobe construction, Spanish builders were using either wood or concrete block.

People who came to look at the progress of the house noticed especially the loving attention to detail. They used hand-wrought hardware as much as possible, laid brick floors, made natural adobe-plastered walls, and built low into the landscape to give

TOP: *Kristina at her loom.*
BOTTOM: *The showroom at Twining Weavers.*

TOP: *Tomasita Duran, veteran weaver at Twining Weavers.* LEFT: *Weaving class at the Pueblo, summer 1967. Jerry, Anita, Julia and Kristina.*

the house the look of belonging where it was like the old Spanish houses. Spanish neighbors dropped in and they felt very complimented when one man commented, "That adobe's pretty beautiful. Maybe I'll put a fireplace like that in my house."

That first house was sold even before it was finished, and when it was done they put their profits back into land, this time out on the mesa west of town where they built a larger house, then another on the land adjoining it when that quickly sold. By this time Kristina had started her Taos Valley Weaving School, which would continue for the next four summers, so she worked on the house construction only part time, doing cabinet work and brick and cement work. Now Meliton Montaño helped Sandy and together they raised beams, built adobe walls—all of the major construction. Meliton was the son of our old benefactress, Mrs. Montaño, who provided us with inspiration and handspun yarn back in the days of the first Craft House.

After the third house sold both Kristina and Sandy went on to other things; Kristina's weaving school continued to occupy her summers, and soon she would become involved in another kind of partnership, a wholesale and retail rug-weaving shop just down the road in Arroyo Seco in an old familiar building. The period of work just finished had been for Sandy a thorough introduction to a general subject that would continue to intrigue and involve her and would result in a book written with her sister Laurel, called *ADOBE! Homes and Interiors of Taos, Santa Fe and the Southwest.*

The Craft House building in Arroyo Seco had sat empty for most of the six years since Rachel closed her business there in 1971. New owners had started projects but none of them had lasted long, and the unused building was beginning to deteriorate. Then one day Kristina was bicycling by and saw Katy Lopez with a crew of men cleaning it up. She went in to say hello and Katy grabbed her by the arm and said, "Kristina—do something with my Craft House!" This dramatic plea, Kristina remembered, hit her "like a thunderbolt" and jogged to the front of her mind a half-formulated plan she had been nursing since the Del Sol job in Truchas—to do something similar nearer home and, most important, independently.

Her friend Christine DiLisio had moved to the valley from Raton, built a house in El Salto, and then started building looms, selling some to Kristina's summer weaving students. Her design was an adaptation from an old Swedish loom of Kristina's and they were especially fine looms. Christine had built a prototype for the McCurdy School in Española, and they had built a number of looms for projects in that area where there were a lot of weavers, near Chimayo.

Excited over her new idea, she had gone right up to talk with Christine, who loved it immediately—and in a very short time they were moving in looms from Kristina's weaving school and setting up Twining Weavers. It was a good partnership of talents. For years Christine had run family businesses in Raton, and she loved the intricacies of bookkeeping and taxes. She made friends with everyone who came in the door and was a fantastic salesperson. Kristina recalled that when customers returned, they would immediately ask for their "friend" if she was not on hand.

There being such a rich tradition of Spanish weaving in the Arroyo Seco area, their plan was to try to involve local people as weavers and this worked out beautifully. Some already wove, others learned and were very good at it, and very soon they had a staff of prodigious workers.

Kristina managed the workshop, ordered materials, and designed the rugs that were their main production item in the bold and vivid colors that had become her trademark as well as in simple natural stripes. Most of their sales were retail, though they had some wholesale accounts, too. They sold to skiers, to tourists, and to local people; and everyone enjoyed the atmosphere of the busy workshop with masses of yarns around and the wonderful simple, modern but definitely southwestern variety of rugs, bags, and pillows that filled much of the space not occupied by looms.

Customers would come in and they would spread out an assortment of yarns and all sit on the floor and discuss room shapes and sizes and colors and plan out the rugs to be woven. One of the largest rugs they made was for the living room of the house I had lived in on the Valdez rim, covering the whole floor. One of the weavers became expert in these huge rugs, joining strips invisibly to make oversize floor coverings.

When a series of rugs was completed, Kristina and the weavers would spread them out and gather around to discuss them and plan the next direction, so the weavers also learned a lot about designing. With managing the overall production, Kristina did very little weaving, and she also relieved Christine sometimes as salesperson. The weavers became very skilled and production continued to increase, as did the business itself. It grew so fast the first year that they realized they could expand to a wholesale business on a grand scale—and perhaps would have been tempted had they begun the project twenty years earlier. But now they were content to keep it small and mostly retail.

After about three years, Christine inherited a business in Capulin from her sister and had to spend part of her time there, tending to that and other family matters, and they had to consider the possibility of selling. Kristina loved the whole project so that she decided to try to go on with it alone, bought Christine out, and continued for almost another year. But she hated the business side of it, spending most of her time on the phone, doing the payroll and the taxes, the selling, instead of the work with yarns and looms that she loved. It was simply too much for one person, and she finally decided to sell it.

Now, ten years after it first opened, Twining Weavers is still a thriving business in Arroyo Seco. And Tomasita Varos, "Tommy," one of the first weavers from the early days, is still weaving there. According to Kristina, "Tommy is the reason the whole thing worked."

Rochelle!

We had not visited Taos for six years, and decided to go west in time for the birth of our first grandchild, expected in September 1977 by Jenny and Pepe (Rochon). The plan was to leave early and drive across Canada to British Columbia, then southeast across the western part of the country that Conor and I had never seen. Conor would miss a little school, but we arranged with his sixth-grade teacher that he would keep a journal of the trip as a substitute for classwork. It was a fine drive of open farmland with vast fields of yellow mustard and of sunflowers between equally large-scale areas of watery wilderness.

Back East, we were beginning to think of living in the country again and had looked for a piece of land there with little success; one objective of this trip was to look at more far-flung possibilities, including Taos Valley, before making a move. David had been impressed with British Columbia when he visited there years before and we found it, indeed, very beautiful. It was spacious, with an interesting contrast of terrain that reminded me a little of New Mexico's mountains, sagebrush land, and intermittent broad valleys of farms and orchards; there was even a reviving Indian culture. We stayed with David's Tweeddale relatives and, with his cousin, explored the country around Salmon Arm in some detail, trying to imagine settling there. Then after a restful interval of fishing a salmon run, exploring mountains, and searching out remote valleys, we headed south, more eager the closer we got to New Mexico. Idaho, Wyoming, and Utah all looked a little like home to me. The high road through the corner of Colorado was still elegant with the last of the golden aspen, but all paled with every mile that brought us closer to the northern border of New Mexico and, finally, we were skimming across the sagebrush desert from Tres Piedras with the mountains and the valley that they encircled in view, over the high Rio Grande bridge and into Taos.

Jenny and Pepe, and the rest of the group that formed the Sterling Smiths, including Seth, Kinlock, and Lorelei, shared a large old adobe hacienda known as the Mabel Dodge house, where Mabel and her husband, Taos Indian Tony Luhan, had lived. On the edge of town, it bordered Indian land on the north and east, and behind it the sagebrush land stretched out to the mountains. It was a wonderful house of large rooms and an atmosphere of old Taos, with carved wood, thick walls, and portals facing a patio and connecting the old house with the rooms of the wings and the shop where everyone worked at their jewelry. Oli had, for some months, been living and working in a studio across the patio from the house, so Conor visited with him, too. Jenny carried her pregnancy beautifully, looking somehow like an elegant blond black woman. We settled into our tiny cedar-lined room—actually a closet large enough to accommodate a bed—and Conor slept on an alcove sofa in the large living room.

This family of young people had created a remarkably well-organized household. The house was clean and orderly and the flow of life very comfortable, with sociability and common life somehow balanced successfully with individuality and privacy. There were usually visitors flowing in and out, and the center of activity was the jewelry shop, where there were usually people working and beautiful things being made. Everyone shared by schedule in shopping and the preparation of meals, which were eaten at one of the large tables in the kitchen or the dining room, all joining hands in a large circle around the kitchen table before eating. The kitchen was well ordered, the food healthy and natural. Periodically there were family meetings to discuss household matters; at one of them it had presumably been decided that we could temporarily join them.

The weeks passed. We visited friends and got reacquainted with the valley. Taos, as usual, had both changed and remained the same. With each return I was amazed at the growth that had taken place—new businesses, an astounding number of new galleries, a variety of new craft shops—much more specialized ones than before, it seemed—a large new courthouse and other public buildings, and new paved roads where, before, there had been dirt lanes. And, of course, population had grown tremendously.

In the "old days" of my longest residence here, the fifties and sixties, it seemed that we were always aware of new arrivals and soon knew who they were and what they were doing. Since that time Taos had ceased to be a small town in that sense. It still *appeared* to be a small and rather simple community, but sheer numbers had divided it into a much more complex society now, even aside from the periodic influx of tourists.

I remembered being surprised, long ago, when John Yaple told us stories of the *really* early days when he arrived in the vallley as a young man in 1925, and wondering that he could absorb all of the changes that had happened. But somehow it is possible; it seems that what we treasure is some mysterious quality that is still here. Privacy and a direct relationship to the landscape still happen.

There was plenty of time to catch up on Kristina and Rachel's activities. Kristina's summer weaving school was going well, with people returning for their second sessions, and we visited her at her Twining Weavers in Arroyo Seco. It was a hive of activity, rows of looms with weavers producing lovely simple rugs and pillows and bags in her distinctive vibrant colors. Her newest enthusiasm, though, was an outdoor one. She had just started her flock of llamas, elegant and aloof creatures that fascinated Conor.

Often David, Conor, and I would walk out through the sage-brush land behind our temporary home and up into the foothills, from where there were good views out over the valley and the desert beyond. There were often potsherds in our path and occasionally a tarantula. One day we were returning home after exploring a canyon, walking single file between low-growing pinons—Conor, then me, then David—when Conor and I saw just ahead a large rattlesnake crossing our trail. We were going at quite a pace, and Conor and I barely managed to stop in time. It collected itself under a low, rangy pinon, and we watched as it coiled, poised for action, and watched us back. We were all fascinated, but David, with an apparently trustful lack of fear, moved closer until he was just out of what he considered its range and conducted a detailed study of it. It apparently decided we were not going to fight, as it uncoiled after a while and straightened out, in position to slither away but still not leaving. David moved closer and closer and slipped a stick under it to test its weight—then, to our horror, reached out and actually touched it as it moved away. Strangely, it seemed that the snake, when it uncoiled but didn't leave, was a little curious also. Conor seemed convinced, however, that he shouldn't try to touch a rattlesnake. The rest of the way down we inspected our path in careful detail, letting David lead the way.

It was always a lovely walk returning from the mountain, particularly in the late afternoon when the land off to the west and up toward Taos Mountain became marked by the shadows gathering in the arroyos as the sunlight slanted low. The late light dramatized the big adobe house and its surrounding tall cottonwoods, the house like an organized extension of the terrain itself, rising three stories to a many-windowed tower room. Then we were in the midst of people and activity again, with dinner about ready.

Conor loved it all—the friendly young adults who included him in things that were going on in a matter-of-fact way, the busy atmosphere, and the work in the jewelry shop. They let him collect the silver filings, which they then weighed and bought from him, and he learned to pound coins into domes for buttons. He went off on wood-cutting expeditions and was even included in a three-day pack trip up to the Villacito saddle, above timberline. In between all of this we conducted his schoolwork on the big dining room table, and he gradually put together a journal of the trip from notes he had made along the way and the maps and brochures we had collected. He made a large map from an atlas Pepe loaned him, and traced our route on it; we collected spelling words from his daily experiences such as *rattlesnake* and *altitude* and *jewelry*.

One afternoon David and I drove west over the new high bridge over the Rio Grande Gorge to explore, and late in the afternoon we happened upon an isolated collection of buildings— house, sheds, and corrals—with a U.S. Post Office sign nailed on the gate post. The house was surprising as, though built of adobe, it was a classic midwestern square house with a centrally-peaked roof and wooden porch placed precisely in the center of its front and a small square yard enclosed by a wire fence. It looked for all the world as though a plains town, now vanished, had once surrounded it.

We had postcards to mail so went in to investigate. Inside

there was a fragrant smell of cooking, and the postmistress appeared from a back room in a friendly bustle, sold us our stamps, and inquired where we were from. We told her we were here to await the birth of a grandchild, and she embarked on stories of the birth of her own children years before. Her husband came in from outdoors and together they told us of one winter when a great snowstorm came up the week before they expected a child to be born, and they bundled up and drove through the blinding snow down to Pilar where they crossed the Rio Grande and then back north to Taos, where she stayed with a sister until her daughter was born. We talked on for half an hour; then when we said we should be getting home she said, as though we were old friends, "Supper is about ready. Why don't you stay?" We were expected for dinner, so declined, but have ever since regretted it.

On October 11 we had a party for Conor's twelfth birthday, then one for Kinlock's, and it became apparent that the expected date for the baby's arrival was optimistic. David needed work to do and took on a barn-building project for Christine DiLisio, for shelter and feed storage for her flock of llamas. So he traveled north every day to the foothills above Arroyo Seco, and with a crew of three women carpenters built a little wooden barn.

Rachel was living in town and was in the last stages of work on her book. In writing the text she had included references to the drawings with which she planned to profusely illustrate it (432 of them). These were important to the book, both for clarity and for general interest, but the actual drawing of them was a mammoth undertaking and fortunately Cheryl Cantu, one of her former apprentices from the Craft House, was able to help her complete them in time for her publishing deadline. She requisitioned Kristina and me to weave some of the samples for the sections of colored photographs. This impressive project of hers was just about ready to go off to the printer and looked very thorough, well researched, and exciting.

Kristina's son, Ian, was home for a visit, the first time I had seen him since he was quite small. He was in college, working on his engineering degree, and usually spent his vacations traveling or exploring—mountain-climbing in Peru, and one summer he spent designing an earthquake-proof house in Guatemala, which David was intrigued to hear about. He spoke Spanish fluently and in South America was usually assumed to be a blond Argentinian. As Kristina said, "He plays vigorously."

Jenny wasn't doing much jewelry work by now, though she and Pepe did make me a pair of earrings—three turquoise drops in silver—and she still worked on drawings for the conchas in the belts that Pepe was making. We worked on sewing for the baby and clothes for her as we waited.

A further distraction was a great Renaissance Fair held in the patio and on the grounds around the house as a benefit for the Taos Music School. There were lavish decorations and costumes, musicians and jugglers and tightrope walkers, a great barbecue, and in the open space out back a hot air balloon was tethered to take people aloft. Just in case, we parked a car by a back drive to the house so we could hurry Jenny to the hospital if the time arrived, but the day passed without need for it. She planned to have the baby at home with the assistance of her midwife and her doctor on call at the hospital, should there be any complications.

Halloween came and we and Jenny took Conor to a party at the house of friends in the village of Arroyo Hondo, arriving home late. The next morning signs of the great event began to happen. When things didn't progress as expected, Tish, the midwife, decided Jenny should go to the hospital after all, and there we waited for what seemed hours until finally waiting turned to celebration, and I got to see my first granddaughter—Rochelle Yasmine Rochon! The birth had finally been by caesarean and Jenny was strained and exhausted, but they both would be fine. Rochelle certainly looked perfect, with lots of dark hair. Back home, Jenny had trouble shaking off an infection and Rachel, Lorelei, I, and others took shifts sleeping in her room and bringing Rochelle to her to nurse during the night. Rochelle grew more beautiful by the hour and was a delight to hold and to watch; Uncle Conor loved to carry her around as she gazed back at him with her dark, dark eyes.

Only a week later we finally had to leave and return to the occupations of our eastern world. We left as the first snow began to fall heavily and were pursued by an east-moving snowstorm all the way across the country. Back home, we were relieved to hear that Jenny had returned to her normal good health and that Rochelle was thriving.

Navajo Country. 65″ × 31″. 1961. Joan Loveless.

Figure. 38″ × 30″. 1962. Joan Loveless.

White Landscape. 55″ × 36″. 1983. Joan Loveless.

Orange Landscape II. 54″ × 36″. 1983. Joan Loveless.

New Landscape. 7′6″ × 36″. 1985. Joan Loveless. Photograph by Chauncey Loomis. Courtesy of Chauncey Loomis Collection.

Interweave: White on White. 67″ × 25″. 1983. Rachel Brown.

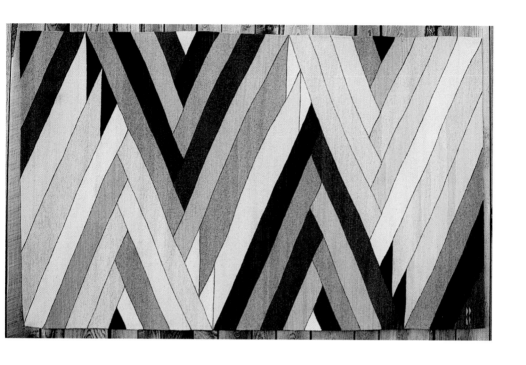

Mauve Interweave. 54″ × 84″. 1986. Rachel Brown.

Point of Departure. 41¹/₂″ × 40″. 1989. Rachel Brown.
Photograph by Rick Mai.

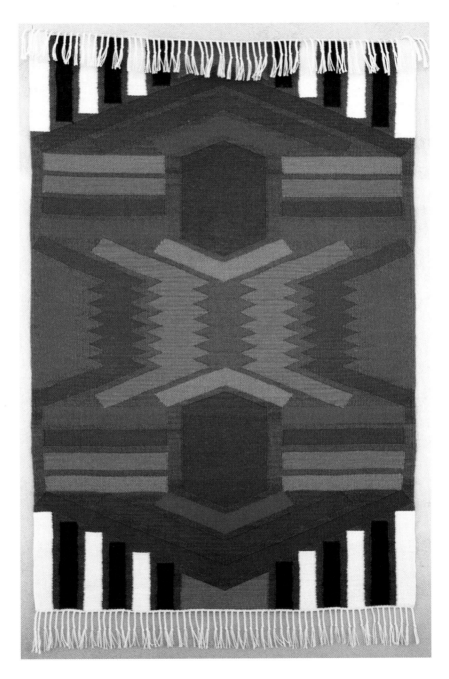

Tribal Symmetry. 59″ × 40¹/₂″. 1990. Rachel Brown.
Photograph by Rick Mai.

Partial Sunlight. 60″ × 41″. 1990. Rachel Brown. Photo by
Rick Mai.

Oasis. 32″ × 40″. 1974. Kristina Wilson.

Sharing 35″ × 31″. 1980s. Kristina Wilson. Photograph by Steve Bradley.

Truth Imprisoned. 43″ × 33″. 1980s. Kristina Wilson.
Photograph by Steve Bradley.

Inadequate Umbrella. 53″ × 43″. 1980s. Kristina Wilson.
Photograph by Steve Bradley.

Olive Branch. 55″ × 36″. 1980s. Kristina Wilson. Photograph
by Steve Bradley.

TOP: Kristina's pillows, Rachel's brushed mohair blanket, and Joan's tapestry, *Horizontal Pinks,* at the opening of a Taos interior design shop in 1964.
BOTTOM: Left to right, Rachel, Kristina, and Joan. 1990.

Pixley Hill

Our store in the village of Housatonic was a wonderful living and working space, but on our wanderings through the countryside we still looked at the land with an eye to finding a piece of it to begin to tend and to dream up a house on, surrounded by the privacy of the country. Because we thought that this third home would be our permanent one, it had to be in the right place and be just the right sort of land.

Then, after looking for miles in every direction, we found just over Pixley Hill, which rose behind us in Housatonic, seventeen acres of lovely land with fine woods and a view out over the next valley. Our thoughts hovered over that land for a while and, finally, we took the plunge and bought it.

These acres became the focus of our thoughts, the site where we would weave all the parts of our life together, a bit of reality spread out that we could inhabit, and through which we could comprehend the time and space of our life and enjoy our place in the scheme of things. I started a journal and its meanderings began, a little giddily with the excitement of discovery, to trace our progress into the land, into our new home.

> *Seventeen acres is quite a lot. Enough to take a while to become acquainted with, enough to leave spots not thoroughly discovered. I remember a composer friend saying that he deliberately resisted getting really to know certain favorite bits of Bach in order to save them as mystery. Here, there is no danger of using up our mysteries very quickly.*
>
> *We usually go over for the last hour before the sun sets, after our work day at the store. Every time we are there the bonds become stronger, we become familiar with another bit of it, see some new beauty, hear the winds blow through our tall*

*pines, get another inkling of the loveliness of the view across
the valley to Tom Ball Mountain which will open up when
we do some clearing of the youngish fat pines that have
grown up in what were once cleared fields divided by a
number of stone walls.*

*The spot we've picked to build our house on is near the
highest point our land reaches on the hill. There are large
birch trees, an old maple now sending out red buds, oaks,
hemlock, and a very tall pine which Conor climbs and which
is supposed to be close enough to his bedroom window for him
to work out some kind of physical communication with it by
rope or bridge. A large boulder lies in what will probably be
our patio and around it the house will face south and
southwest with many windows to take in the sun and an
inner fireplace wall of stone to absorb and store the warmth
for us. Behind us is a vast stone, the visible part of it bigger
than our kitchen at home, which David thinks it would be
fine to dig a root cellar up against. Now Conor has added
that to the "definite plan" collection. Just over the tumbled
remains of a stone wall is a quite level meadow in which we
have been subduing a blackberry thicket in preparation for a
garden. We just set out a row of Concord grapevine cuttings
from our arbor in town across the top of that clearing.*

Another early entry:

*Yesterday's work produced a visible channel where the
road will start its gradual climb beside great trees, around
sizable boulders. Today we will finish that, clearing the
thorny tangles so we can walk easily all the way to The
Site. Conor likes this clearing—he's having a marvelous
time, incredulous at our audacity yet happily believing that
we can build a house, and even a barn. It amazes us that we
have found such a wilderness tract so nearby.*

*We have wandered a number of possible routes and have
finally settled on what appears to be the path of least
resistance, a gradual rise without crossing especially lovely
spots which are best left alone. This criss-crossing exploration
begins to make the land a little familiar. One day David
found what appear, though they have no leaves yet, to be low*

blueberry bushes and just beyond them a high blueberry. At this stage we find, lose, and find again these treasures. The old stone walls are confusing; one suddenly appears and we don't know whether it borders the second or third field. We are torn between an urge to get the lay of the land and delight in discovering and losing track again.

All that spring and summer we spent our spare time in clearing, planning, and getting acquainted with the land, carrying tools, water, and food for picnics up the hill. One day in the midst of a particularly hard day of clearing, we were sitting amongst our stacks of brush and logs, resting and looking out through the new openings we had made to the view. An elderly man appeared slowly out of the trees below us, walking with a sapling cane, and after introductions stood with us a long time, one hand over the other on the head of his cane in what we came to know as his resting posture, and told us the story of our land.

Forty years before, he had come to the area to work on the farm of which our acres were a part. He swung his arm around to take in everything below him on the hill and said, "I had it all in corn." The stone walls were already there then, probably for many years. When the owner, a woman, became elderly and ill his wife nursed her and, when she died, the land was all left to him. It was hard to believe that all of those trees had grown up in fifteen yers, but he assured us that it was quite true.

Conor had a quick eye and wide vision for wildlife and often we would hear his shout to us as he caught fleeting glimpses of the wild residents of the land on his wanderings. Often he saw disappearing foxes as tawny blurs between the trees. Once when I was with him we both caught sight of one of these, a strange visual experience seeing the *disappearance* of something. You know that you have seen something, but only long enough to identify its presence by its immediately following absence, its color by a sense of a color missing, which you are conscious of just having noticed and its movement by the fact that it just caught your attention.

He reported that we had wild turkeys on the land, over near the last meadow; they had risen from the ground with their strange and wonderful cry and disappeared into the trees. I had no difficulty in sharing the image of that sight as I remembered clearly

the particular character of their hurrying diagonal takeoff and
gobble from the woods of my childhood; the gobble always sounded
to me as though it came from inside their wings. Soon we came
to matter-of-factly accept Conor's sightings and knew that what
he saw we would most likely eventually see, too.

That summer we entered the land at the lowest corner where
it fronted on Pixley Hill Road, parked our truck in the clear
meadow, and then walked through the woods. When we first
went there regularly, ferns were just beginning to send up their
tightly curled leaf shoots between the boulders of the stone wall
and all across the land budding things stood out clearly. As that
summer progressed, the spaces between those distinct buds filled
in quickly as leaf grew to meet leaf and, in the lower field, the
spring carpet of green gradually rose to a height of two feet or
more, and we had to work at tramping and pulling the weeds to
keep a path through it.

Through the summer we watched the succession of buds and
blooms and leaves then, finally, the varied brilliance of the turning
of the leaves and the return to bare branches, the earth carpeted
with a different set of colors and the only green remaining, those
of the mossy stones and the evergreens. Then the tall trees seemed
taller, the structure of the forest more clear. Flocks of geese passed
over often, their V's pointing south, and our planning began to
focus on what we would do when the next spring came. We
watched the weather clues in the sky differently now—would it
soon snow? There was an air of suspense in the woods now as
though all of the living things there, seen and unseen, were ex-
pectantly bracing themselves, had already begun their next season
and would manage quite well without us. Bundled up, we carried
to the truck the bigger wood that had been drying since the early
clearing and took it home and were consoled by the comfort it
produced. Perhaps by the next winter we would not have to leave
our woods when the leaves fell and the wind blew cold.

❿ ❿ ❿

Through the winter we were content with working at the
store and planning the spring work to be done on the land. Then
the following summer outdoor work resumed; but when we began to build our house it was in a spot lower on the land, in an

open meadow with tall hickories, maples, and oaks standing by the stone wall on one side and wild apple trees bordering the other, a place we had named Apple Field when we tramped through it each trip up the hill. Somehow we couldn't settle on a place for a house up there; each spot seemed perfect as it was, and we decided that our temporary residence there had served its purpose, had given us the sense of privacy we needed, the feel of the depths of the land and that lower down the road was the spot that could be successfully inhabited. Even there much clearing needed to be done and we ranged up and down and around the meadow like goats nibbling away a bit here and a bit there, clearing a building site; then one day we discovered the blueberry bushes that we had found once and then lost again, conveniently just at the side of what would be our yard.

The house was to be set into the hillside, the basement to become studio at ground level in the front and above it the living floors to be built in the two following summers. When the second fall came the basement construction was done, and the following summer we moved into it and continued to build upstairs. It was a busy time for David, supervising the building of houses that he designed and bringing the crew to the land during lulls in other construction. I went over the hill to weave at the store when there was time and then finally was able to move my looms to the land and really get back to work.

Weaving a Tapestry

This new house was a wonderful setting for work, surrounded by woods and open to the valley below us, with Tom Ball Mountain beyond. I enjoyed the isolation and quiet away from the village. Just up the stairs was my kitchen and there I dyed up batches of yarn, then draped them on a drying rack in the shade outdoors. For this first piece I dyed up a fine array of oranges. Joan Erikson wrote me that she was working on a new book, to be called *Wisdom and the Senses,* and asked if I could write something for her describing the process of weaving one of my tapestries, to be used in the book. I said I would try, keeping it in mind as I worked on the piece I had just started, and the following was the result.

◐ ◐ ◐

When I am weaving in the morning and the work is going well—images building and tantalizing drifts and hints of the forms to come darting past—my mind races here and there, to other projects, other materials and forms, and I have to pull it back to weaving. My energy is high, cello music on the radio is soaring and delving, and the shapes I'm working on are beginning shapes and could go anywhere. Also, my mind plucks at this and that string to avoid finalizing the shapes I'm working on too soon, to keep the choices open and let the paths the weaving takes remain free for longer—to find the other alternative, the not-yet-seen way.

My mind in its flight sees my lovely granddaughter, Rochelle, and a tapestry for her begins. I see a kind of veiled surface rising, a surface of naturals back and forth horizontally—a lighter, a slightly darker or different tone—

116

and, as though the weaving is a web, I part it here and there and rounded shapes appear in the openings, perhaps clear light blues, the unknown of her life. I must weave it for her soon; I'll start spinning for it—naturals—and dreaming up the blues.

Now I know I've started to weave again. Across my loom are two orange shapes building and between them are three pale to rich golden brown shapes, one turning back to orange by way of a bit of rosy brick color to make the end of the tan less final. As I work, a wonderful thing is happening which I didn't know I was missing. All the areas across the weaving are building at once. I bring one up a few rows and as I glance away to look at one on the far side of the warp I am caught unawares just enough to realize what really should be done next on the one I looked away from and a good new turn for the shape to take occurs to me. And suddenly I realize that this is what has been missing—this interdependence of the parts, this getting involved in the part of the part—building the shapes not as solids (things) *but as growing events. So I continue working across my warp keyboard, five small balls of yarn lying on the free warp. I had been impatient, wanting to complete a shape, a decision, until I realized that this was precisely what I needed, what had been missing—this flowing back and forth to build the whole and keeping the communication open between the parts—truly open.*

Tapestry weaving has the built-in difficulty that one can work on only one level at a time, the weaving progressing across the entire width, from the bottom (usually) *to the top. I can weave only so far with a form before I must go back and bring up the rest of the total before going ahead. Since I don't use cartoons, don't usually in any concrete way design ahead, my images are purely "perhaps" images which actually determine the* direction *I go in. My drawings are exercises, almost like playing scales, establishing a visual mood and perhaps sketching a particular* shape problem *that I want to deal with. Often it happens, though, that the shape problem or visual mood that I begin with does not appear till some later tapestry, or it becomes transformed into a variation which becomes more intriguing and with which I work instead.*

When I had just begun this tapestry, working in rich close oranges and deep reds, I had put in some bits of lavender and a bit of light blues and at the end of the day my son, Conor, came in when the weaving was dropped down for looking at the day's work. He said, "Wow, I like those blips of color—but don't do too much of them now!" So that was a good clue that I was on the right track.

I've spun most of the yarn for this tapestry, partly because I seem to have an immense supply of raw wool around the studio. But mostly I'm spinning it to get immersed in it. It's been a long time since I've woven and I need to spin my way into it. First I dyed up a batch of oranges, brewing and mixing skeins in several pots, trying to get many steps of orange—rosy ones, bright light ones, rusty ones, and some browned enough to be close to a few brownish reds I'm going to use. What I'm really after is colors that I can't easily name—strange colors. It's good when I can't predict just how they'll look when they are together, which direction they'll go in. Then they demand real attention and direct their own handling and create surprises for me, leading me where I had not planned to go. This is what I really like—having something happen in the weaving that I didn't expect and having to really study it and figure out how to use it—how to pick up on it if it is intriguing and find the direction it will lead me in.

Problems usually come up. In this, I'm weaving along playing five or six oranges together, absorbed in their small differences and building beginning shapes. Toward the end of the day I'm tired, having used up my eyes, and suddenly realize that I've gotten into the trap of unrelieved orange. All those luminous colors are darkening. I've run out of leavening and take two days off from weaving to spin. I need a slightly colored neutral, maybe a faintly dyed bluish color. I spin directly from the fleece, without carding, so the yarn will take the dye unevenly and the color even more faintly. My spinning wheel faces the loom and I can keep the weaving in view as I spin. It still looks problematical, though a night's sleep has rid my eyes of the overdose of looking at orange.

After I dye a few skeins of faint bluish, I realize that that won't work and put it aside for later. The solution turns out to be a very lightly dyed combination of golden brown and dark brown. I spin more and go back to the loom with two batches of faint warm colors, one with a bit more brown and one a bit more golden. It's always good to use little enough dye; this literally took only a few sprinkles of dye powder. Usually when I'm dyeing I get carried away with the colors and dye some that don't fit into the piece I'm working on and I set them to the side to wait their turn. I like that, as my mind begins to work secretly on them and I gradually add to them as I do up batches of yarn.

When I went back to the tapestry I wasn't at all sure it would work and had prepared myself for cutting the warp, unraveling the weaving, and beginning again. But it did work! The light, slight colors immediately breathed air into the oranges, combining with them for a while and then opening into a totally light area for a while before bringing the oranges in again, gradually. It's been a good working week. I've been able to start working early when my attention is clearest and to work long days, blending spinning, dyeing, and weaving, which helps all three. I work hard to keep the neutrals active. Now that they're in they have to hold their own or they'll slip into background and I don't want that.

One of the things that I have to work hard at is to diminish the discrepancy between the imagined image and the final produced image. Often I have seen clearly a beautiful form that I wanted to weave—get just a glimpse of it—and then set out to execute it and find my image gone, or not what I thought it to be. It may be that the problem is in not examining the image carefully enough to understand it, in trying to make the jump from a subtle thought to a constructed image too suddenly. Perhaps I leave out steps and therefore lose it. I must learn to gradually nurture it and go through the stages of mentally interpreting it—of materializing it before subjecting it to the difficulties of being actually reproduced in materials, yarns. In the mind the image had an environment—mood, thoughts that preceded it, even what one was doing when the image presented itself. All

119

these were part of the circumstance of the image and even if it is a workable idea it needs clarifying, isolating, to check whether it is an idea or a reaction.

Finally the piece is done and it does indeed stand on its own. When a tapestry is successful I can study it and finally realize what has gone on in it. Then it makes its link to the next one. Curiosities are evoked by it which create a next beginning, not necessarily related in color or even in form, but while the process of working with the phenomena of that tapestry is still fresh in my mind I peruse it for those set-aside thoughts that came and went as I worked. And I find suggestions of shapes, of mood, of color when the work is ended and hung on the wall that set me going again.

Crisis

I n the spring of 1980 I flew out to New Mexico to spend two weeks with Jenny and Rochelle, who was then two and a half years old. Jenny and Pepe had parted, and the girls and Lorelei were living in Lorelei's grandmother Lesley's small basement apartment in Taos with her garden outside their door and a jewelry workshop in her garage. Rochelle had grown wonderfully since their last visit with us in Massachusetts; she was now a tiny, energetic sprite with lots to say and still with those velvety dark eyes. It was my first visit to the valley since Rochelle was born, and I had a wonderful time seeing friends and catching up on things there.

Rachel was, as usual, extremely busy with weaving and spinning. She had, the year before, a show of her work at Clay and Fiber Gallery in Taos, for which she wove a group of her new "diagonal tapestries." She told me the story of how these had come about. When her daughter, Lorelei, was about fourteen, she and a friend wanted to learn to spin and weave, so Rachel taught them at the Craft House, and they produced several lovely handspun rugs that were sold there. Then she taught Lorelei the tapestry technique and when ready to begin her own piece, Lorelei had sat at her loom with her hands lying on the warp, fingertips interlocked, trying to think of a design to weave—and then began to weave the pattern that her fingers were making, a series of interlocking curves and stripes. It turned out to be a very successful piece and Rachel was intrigued with it. Ever since, she had planned to continue with studying this pattern, and for this show she did—the forms changing to interlocking triangles rather than curves—and she wove a whole series of them.

Her Rio Grande spinning wheel was in production now, and her new project was a spinning business with John Ussery. John had set up a carding machine at his home up on the mountainside near El Rito, south of Taos. She dyed wool in a range of colors and then designed mixtures of them, which he carded together in his machine, then she spun up the yarn on her new wheel for marketing.

She was buying her wool from a supplier in Brady, Texas, a major sheep-raising area, and the wool was shipped in great six-hundred-pound bales. Once she ordered two of these large bales, and she and her son, Seth, picked up the shipment in his truck and dumped them in the small parking lot by her house in Taos. Seth unbuckled the metal bands that compressed them, and with a great "pfhhht" they sprang free to fill the whole space from wall to house. The wool was then bagged and stored in a shed, gradually dyed for the blends she was making, carded on John's machine in El Rito, then all spun by Rachel—an incredible amoung of spinning. She got so skilled that she could spin three pounds of this heavy yarn in an hour.

Later, when Kristina was running Twining Weavers, Rachel spun this yarn for the weaving there, once in a marathon project of 250 pounds each of three colors, when she remembers feeling like the miller's daughter in Rumpelstiltskin in the midst of bags of pink and rust and gold wool, spinning madly for days on end to complete an order before leaving to teach a spinning workshop in Aspen, Colorado.

Rachel's book was doing very well. It was selected as a Book-of-the-Month-Club alternate, and the response to it was gratifying, though her dream of retiring to "just weave" was not quite realized.

Kristina was busy with her building projects, getting ready for another session of her tapestry-weaving school, and taking care of her llama flock, which had grown considerably. We hadn't really talked since her summer school had become an established thing, and I was interested in hearing how she went about teaching tapestry weaving. She taught that particular technique because it was little taught at the time, but more because it was her particular way of working, the kind of weaving that she almost always did, in some form. She wove bags and pillows "just to make a living," but her real love had always been tapestry or "weft-faced" weaving as it had traditionally been done in southwestern weaving, both Spanish and Indian, with the weft covering the warp entirely as is usual in rugs.

She limited her students to seven or eight so that they could work more individually and yet still get together at times to share as a group. She taught loom mechanics so that people would understand *why* things worked the way they did and had each student put at least two warps on a loom during the session, as simply as possible, as she wanted them to feel familiar and at ease with the loom and the mechanics of weaving. She said that the students came into the class with a whole set of inhibitions such as, "I can't understand anything mechanical," and "I don't have any artistic ability," and sometimes also, "My teacher said you're supposed to do it this way," whereas she wanted them to go out with a comprehension of *how* and *why* things were done. She also wanted them to experience the building of shapes in the simplest terms so that they could use this basic knowledge freely in designing their own weaving. Her method really seemed to work. In learning the tapestry technique in this step-by-step way—first building one color, then two, then forming diagonals, then on to more complicated shapes and arrangements—the students became free to design because they had first mastered the basic means of construction.

The students, who came from various parts of the country, camped by or stayed in Kristina's house and worked so intently that she had trouble even getting them out for walks or down to the river to swim. They worked early and late and produced great quantities of weaving; some of them, when they got back home, sold pieces they had made during the summer and thus paid for their weaving course.

Jenny and Lorelei were planning to come east for a while and when it was time for me to leave, Jenny and I decided at the last moment that Rochelle should fly back with me and she and Lorelei follow in a few weeks. Our plane was to arrive late at night, and David decided to surprise Conor with Rochelle's arrival and managed to set up her bed in his room after he was asleep, then went to meet us. We deposited her there quietly on our return, and he was indeed surprised to see his little niece in the morning.

We were living in the basement of our new house and enjoying introducing Rochelle to the first events of spring there when the serene rhythm of our life on the land was interrupted by the

discovery that I might have to have cancer surgery. I suppose I
was in the best possible situation to face such a crisis, but still it
cut clear through the fabric of our lives and, a year later, when I
wrote the following in my journal, the digesting of the experience
was still going on.

> *I went into the hospital for tests and confidently awaited
> results. On Mother's Day David, Conor, and Rochelle
> brought me a bouquet of all the wild flowers that had begun
> to bloom. But optimism or no, it was determined that I
> would have to have a mastectomy and remain incarcerated for
> another two weeks.*
>
> *I can't now remember that time as two weeks. Being a
> basically well person, I was soon up and around part of the
> time and had my family's daily visits and flowers and
> assurances from friends that others they had known had been
> through it and all had turned out well, so my spirits were
> good and I accepted what I couldn't change, had a nice rest
> and was well taken care of. Jenny came early from New
> Mexico and took over with her magic household touch, much
> to David's relief. While I was resting in regal ennui he had
> been carrying on all his work accompanied by Rochelle and
> he and Conor were happy to turn over the home-keeping to
> her.*
>
> *When I left the hospital it was surprising to see the trees
> leafed out; it really did then seem that I'd been gone a long
> time. The house was full of flowers—somehow David,
> Jenny, and Conor had made the move upstairs and my top-
> floor bedroom was a welcome haven with its view over the
> valley.*
>
> *So there I was, only two weeks later, with my world
> changed in some shocking way which I soon learned I would
> not be able to fully assimilate for a long time. The surgery
> was successful, I was rid of the cancer, but after I was back to
> somewhat normal strength I had to begin a long program of
> preventive chemotherapy, a two-year course of treatment.
> Now that is almost halfway behind me and I've learned to
> live with it pretty well, designing my life around it. The plot
> was to have injections for a period of five days and then six
> weeks in which to recover from them. After several such*

periods I realized that the reason for the spacing was that the effect of the medication lasted for that long and that in the last week I would begin to feel quite normal, just in time to begin again.

I was determined to find a workable way of living with it, but for the first six months I was simply dominated by it. I took lots of vitamins on the theory that my body needed all the help it could get to achieve some kind of normalcy under the chemical barrage. The doctors persist in claiming that a good normal diet is all that's needed, but I felt that when I kept to the vitamins I felt better sooner and the one period when I neglected to take them was the only time that my blood count was low.

At first all I could do comfortably was reading, certainly a pleasant activity for which I didn't ordinarily have enough time. I decided to make that a structured project and started reading history. It really was a luxury to be able to pursue a subject and the worst symptoms were held at bay when my mind was absorbed. The chemotherapy seems to put a subtle pressure on one's head, an almost intangible feeling of unwellbeing that keeps one from being able to work and live normally, to feel and think normally.

As the year has passed the time that I feel unwell has become shorter. I decided to try to weave a tapestry and got my loom warped with fresh linen warp, spun yarn when I could, and had everything ready to begin weaving when my good weeks arrived. It was marvelous to work again and I finished a tapestry before Christmas. To my surprise the tapestry was different from those that I wove before. I had really labored on it and as I went along could not tell at all if it was going to be successful.

It had been so long since I had worked and there was a real sense of struggle; I was determined to finish it before the next treatments began, whether it would turn out to be a good piece or not. I hadn't consciously worked differently or aimed for a different kind of image, but the result was somehow distinctly different. There was a dramatic tension in it, a boldness, a strength, that had not been there before.

I have woven tapestries for more than twenty years and it seemed that this was the way I could digest the shock, the turmoil, the reality of my life and the turn it had taken. As I looked at this new piece I saw that the quality of my life had indeed changed and the earlier tapestries seemed an expression of that old life when I invented problems—challenges—in order to subdue them, when my work was serene, balanced, a peaceful counterpoint. I liked the new element and found myself feeling happy to have discovered this gutsier side of life.

I used the same sorts of materials, worked with the same sorts of forms basically, but somehow I let them get rougher, occasionally more precipitous—pushed them further before resolving them in finishing the tapestry. It was as though I was finally incorporating the reality of my life as it had become, including the pain and discomfort, the fragility and vulnerability, into my consciousness through this medium of weaving. I had not been able to write about it, really, but the abstractness of the weaving and the long familiarity of it simply became a vehicle for honestly reacting to change, by-passing the conscious resistances.

A life-threatening situation is bound to alter all of one's deeper attitudes and values, one's goals and priorities. Now, I find that my feelings, my convictions, are more outspoken. I'm more determined to test out my life, to discover what is important, to find my voice. There is apparently a freeing element in accepting trauma, in experiencing deep daily fear, in grasping the more threatening side of reality. It is as though one becomes freed from ghosts by facing demons, that one gains strength by surviving a battle, by involuntarily coming face to face with the dark side of life. I suppose that we know it is there and have lived, on some level, in dread of encountering it, have thought we could evade it by designing our lives cleverly, by selective living. At any rate, it is somehow fascinating to enter the Real World where there may be Trouble; there is a kind of beauty in the contrast. When one has felt one's physical self harmed, there is a new pungency in the experience of feeling good; one feels more well than ever before when feeling well at all.

So I continue my struggle to be well, to force my days to fit my intentions, to feel in some measure in control of my immediate destiny. Gone is the old casualness with which I relegated much to the vague future. When I have energy, it cries out to be used and when I don't I take satisfaction in inventing an energyless way to accomplish something and become totally immersed in trying to grasp the intricacies of ancient history. Sometimes I feel a little afraid that this state of physical affairs will become habitual, that when the remaining year is over I won't remember any more how to be normal, but now that I have a month at a time with no drastic symptoms, I feel already like my old self again, so I guess the system will remember.

This winter has been a grandly cold one which has by and large been a pleasure. Last winter never really arrived, which fitted beautifully with the stage of our building, but we missed the drama of real winter. David had other work that prevented him from working on the house and we finally had to abandon the fireplace construction and connect up the old iron parlor stove that we used in Housatonic, and that and the wood-burning kitchen stove have kept us warm with the help of our many south windows; it has been clear cold rather than cloudy cold.

There have been family events of a totally positive sort, also. I was up, last summer, just in time to attend Kimry and John Griffen's wedding at the little church in Housatonic, a lovely and happy ceremony. Lorelei came to join Jenny and they decided to stay in the East for a while in a small house in Housatonic which suits them well. Rochelle enjoys her house and small yard and the goings-on of the village that pass by her doorway. She often sleeps at our house and now it is her other home. And David's son, Keith, spends much time in Lorelei's company, so we are watcing that possible weaving together of families—and Rachel will be arriving soon for a visit with the girls.

A month ago tentative budding began and we took Rochelle around to inspect the buds so she could properly appreciate the leaves coming out. Then chilly days returned and spring stood suspended for weeks, but now leafing out has resumed, our daffodils are blooming and the catkins are bright rose on the maple trees. The squirrels are collecting last fall's hickory nuts from the ground where they have been frozen in and I'm glad to have the winter behind me.

Tierra Wools

L ooking west from Taos, the desert, with the slash of the Rio Grande gorge cutting across it and the dark green of the isolated single peaks rising here and there from its floor, finally meets the far mountains that form the western horizon, blue and indistinct as to features. These are the San Juan Mountains. Just north of Taos the highway takes off to the west, crosses the gorge on the new Rio Grande bridge with the river breathtakingly far below it and continues to Tres Piedras, a bit of a crossroads village, then climbs into the San Juans and travels on their heights for some fifty miles, finally descending into another great valley system on the other side at the village of Tierra Amarilla.

Just beyond that lies the even smaller village of Los Ojos, which in the fall of 1982 became part of Rachel's orbit. Loraine Mooney, with whom she had worked in the Mountain and Valley Wool Association (MAVWA), introduced her to Maria Varela; over lunch Rachel heard about Maria's work and plans for the communities in the Los Ojos area and how Rachel might fit into those plans.

Maria, a teacher at the University of New Mexico, an expert in economic and social development, and an activist in civil rights and the organization of cooperatives, was, with the sheep growers of the Los Ojos area, forming a cooperative enterprise to revitalize the agricultural economy of that part of northern New Mexico. She had lived near Los Ojos for many years while organizing and directing a medical clinic for that economically depressed Hispanic community and shared the local farmers' concern that outside land development in the valley was a threat to their grazing and water resources. In an area primarily devoted to sheep ranching the cooperative—*Ganados del Valle* (Livestock Growers of the Valley)—was formed to cooperatively graze their sheep, market their lambs, and sell their wool, enabling them to compete with the larger ranches and other outside development interests and thereby hold their own in this valley, the home of their ancestors.

These ancestors arrived from Mexico in the late 1700s, bringing with them a breed of sheep called Churro. Through the 1800s when the area was part of Mexico and later when New Mexico was annexed as a Territory of the United States, the economy revolved around sheep and weaving. Los Ojos was remote, separated by the San Juans from the Rio Grande valley, but it was a rich area of high mountain pastures, wooded land, and lower arable land. Water filled the rivers year-round from the melting snows in the mountains. Ditches, laboriously dug by hand, brought irrigation water to the flat lower pastures and fields, the same ditches that are maintained today as the vital source of life in the valley. Thousands of sheep were taken to the high mountain meadows to graze for the short three-month summer. Eight-foot snows and fierce winds make the mountain roads impassable for three to five months of the winter, even today.

Maria and Rachel hit it off immediately, and in their first meeting in Taos dreamed up many possible plans, deciding that the best beginning would be some kind of spinning cottage industry, using the locally grown wool. They arranged to next meet in Los Ojos so that Rachel could look over the situation, and as they parted Maria said enthusiastically, "Let's just start—willy nilly!" and Rachel responded, "We can call it Wooly Nilly Yarns!"

Rachel found the drive from Taos spectacular, the last fifty miles high in the mountains and then, with the huge rock cliffs of Los Brazos (The Arms) standing like a sentinel over it, a vast valley spread out before her. In Los Ojos she met Maria, who took her around to meet some of the growers and their families, who showed her their sheep.

Many were the standard black-faced Suffolk and a Columbia-Rambouillet cross. But her spinner's eye also picked out some with longer-tipped wool and she was told that these were the *Navajosos* or Churro. The grower, Gumercindo, told them that his mother had never let him sell any of those for meat even though their fleece brought less money from the wool broker. Her reasons were sentimental; they were the sheep that had "always been in her family." They were of the original breed and in the isolation of this valley had remained relatively pure.

The wool of these Churro sheep was of a very high quality for spinning. They had long, lustrous, silky, and nearly greaseless fibers in an unusual range of colors—black, apricot, brown, silver, and champagne as well as white. Their black fleece kept its blackness under the intense southwestern sun, whereas the black wool of most other breeds became bleached on the surface of the fleece.

They visited *La Clinica,* the medical clinic that Maria had helped to found, and there Rachel saw a small exhibition of weavings done by some local women. One in particular, woven by a woman named Kika Chavez, though of synthetic yarn, struck her with its strong, original images, and she began to think of the revival of weaving in the valley as well as spinning.

They made plans to begin with a spinning workshop as soon as possible, and a few weeks later Maria called to tell her that she had raised money to buy one of Rachel's Rio Grande Spinning Wheels and that a group was ready for the workshop. When she drove over the mountains again, the aspen trees had turned to gold; winter was not far away.

The response to the workshop was surprising. There were about fifteen participants, including several men, who in the Hispanic tradition also spun and wove. The people who came had all either done some spinning, using the traditional *malacate,* or handspindle, or had seen their mothers or grandmothers spin. Some even brought a supply of already carded wool. They were amazed at the speed with which they could produce yarn on the wheel as compared with the handspindle.

The workshop was held in an old convent building next to the church where Kika and some of the other women worked in a small room on old looms built as part of a HELP project. The looms were in poor shape and the materials mostly synthetic yarns, but these women had indeed already begun to work.

Plans grew through the winter. They would work with Ganados del Valle to improve the wool-growing techniques in the valley, and with this wool they would produce weavings and sell them from their own retail outlet. Then early in the spring before the pass over the mountains was free of snow and open to traffic, Rachel started driving the long southern way around the mountains to Los Ojos, and the dreams began to take form in reality.

The first thing they did was to take all the cotton warps off the looms and replace them with wool ones. And Cruz, the local loom maker, made them a warping board. Before, the women had made their warps by walking back and forth down the unheated hall from one of their rooms to the other.

While Maria was working on a proposal to get a grant for a revolving loan fund with which the women could buy better equipment and a supply of wool warp yarns, the women set to work. The very first weaving made with a weft of 100 percent natural local wool handspun and woven in a tapestry technique came off Rosalia Chacon's loom, and Kika learned how to beam a thirty-yard soft warp of ten threads to the inch with which to weave warp-faced *ruanas* (open-fronted ponchos). A few young women who had no weaving or spinning experience joined the group and were trained from the beginning. Then they had their first Dyeing Day and from that moment on all the yarns that weren't natural colors were hand-dyed.

Space was becoming a serious problem, not only for work space but for a retail outlet where the products that had been woven could be offered for sale. Money was being raised for materials, but the weavers were to be paid from the sale of their work. The priest assured them that they could continue to use the convent rooms, and volunteer church workers would help with remodeling, but the space would not accommodate the growth of the project that was already beginning to happen.

There were plenty of vacant buildings on the main street of Los Ojos, and Rachel was convinced that with a good, visible location, the sale of weavings would pay for a modest rent. The only business in town was a small grocery in the front of an otherwise empty large building, and they visited that first. For Rachel it was a déjà-vu experience. The layout of the front room was exactly like her old Craft House in Arroyo Seco, with large front windows and a door inset into the center, high ceilings, and the walls lined with shelves and bins; the whole space was almost sixty feet long and thirty wide.

When they asked about renting a vacant room, the proprietress said, "Well, I'm closing down the grocery on Friday and we're putting the building up for sale." Rachel and Maria exchanged amazed glances; even though the building was in poor repair, it had the makings of an ideal studio and retail showroom with plenty of space for wool storage and for expansion as their project grew. Later, when David and I visited the showroom and heard the story, we were struck by the similarity to our own experience back in Massachusetts when we took over and renovated the old hardware store, also with high ceilings and shelf-lined walls, into a spacious workshop-showroom. We, too, had inquired about renting and had been told, "Well, I might want to sell."

Their decision to buy the building was almost unavoidable. Money was raised to make a down payment, and in July they had their grand opening with floors sanded and walls and ceilings freshly painted by the volunteer church workers. Six looms, newly built by Cruz, were lined up along the walls, along with spinning wheels. New weavings were on display: rugs, ruanas, pillows; handspun, fleecy throws; and even some small tapestries. Small foundations, churches, and individuals had contributed to getting things started, having faith that with a little help the enterprise would flourish. The opening coincided with a centennial celebration of the San Jose parish, and a centennial weaving—a tapestry depicting the church—was woven by Rosalia and donated to the church in appreciation of their help in housing the beginnings of the project.

Tierra Wools seemed an appropriate name since the larger, better-known, nearby town was named Tierra Amarilla (Yellow Land). Los Ojos had originally been the hub of business in the area, hence the large vacant buildings, but Tierra Amarilla became the county seat and Los Ojos became just one of several population clusters around it.

So they were officially open for a cooperative manufacturing and marketing business, not yet using all locally grown wool, but at least all American wool. The Rio Grande Wool Mill, fifty miles back across the mountains in Tres Piedras, started up about this same time, and by the spring of 1984 Tierra Wools began to buy their wool there. The mill was another manifestation of the integration of the wool industry in the area that had been coaxed along by WAVWA (originally Wool Products Association or WPA), and the two wool businesses benefited each other. The mill spun a lovely singles (one-ply) yarn that was very much like the original handspun yarn used in Rio Grande blankets a century before. Rachel felt that things were beginning to tie together and that follow-through on tradition was all-important.

Immediately, the problems of getting started were replaced by those of structure and organization and general functioning.

The original intention was to have the loan fund go toward purchase of looms and yarns and have the weavers paid from actual sales of their work. But she and Maria saw that the project would fall apart unless the women started making some money right away, however little. Rio Arriba is one of the poorest counties in the United States. Also, the bookkeeping for such an arrangement would have been overwhelming. Molly, one of the new young weavers, had become the bookkeeper and she agreed with them, so they arranged to pay the weavers as soon as a piece was completed satisfactorily. Quality control was up to Rachel and her approval slip was required for a weaver to be paid.

Then an even bigger problem presented itself. The weavers didn't understand why they received only $30 for a rug that sold for $135. Rachel explained her pricing formula, which allowed for materials, labor (by the piece, as an incentive to fast weavers), studio expenses (rent, utilities, communal equipment, insurance, and so forth), and mark-up (to cover bookkeeping, selling supplies, and other hidden expenses). All this added up to the wholesale price. The full retail price would be double this, allowing them to wholesale for 50 percent off, the "keystone" principle that most retailers prefer. When customers bought directly from the workshop showroom, they were given a 25 percent studio discount from the full retail. This they were able to do because they were manufacturing and selling out of the same space and usually weren't so busy that the salesperson couldn't also be doing other jobs.

Still, the pricing was an absolute mystery to many and rumors started in the village that Tierra Wools was a place where women were working for practically nothing, and someone was making a lot of money. Rachel kept explaining that there was no "someone" who was making a lot of money because *they* owned the business, and they were the only *they* there was. Maria had raised money from private funds to pay Rachel as consultant and teacher and for the revolving loan fund. Beyond that, they were on their own; the rent (or building payments) had to be made as well as utilities, insurance, equipment, office supplies, interest (and eventually principal) on the revolving loan.

From the beginning, a certain number of hours of volunteer work each week were required of the weavers in order to buy into the co-op—work such as shop tending, janitorial jobs, sorting and shelving yarns, ordering and shipping and, later, management jobs such as coordinating production and marketing. In addition, there was a minimum production requirement each month. The group voted to require these commitments of any weaver who wanted to qualify as a member-owner, eligible for profit-sharing in the future.

The first year was monumentally difficult in many ways—deciding what to produce, ordering supplies, and trying to keep quality control while encouraging experience—and one of Rachel's most demanding jobs was trying to convince the women that they had a good thing going and that *eventually* they would make money. The first year's business was shaky at best, with people still learning how to weave and spin, none of them with any previous business experience, and making very little money. In the early spring months sales did not equal the payroll, and paychecks were delayed. All of this discouraged production to such an extent that the retail shop was nearly out of stock by mid-August.

But somehow they got through it, and the second year achieved a 300 percent increase in gross, the third year a 75 percent increase with a good bank balance at year's end to last through the lean spring months. They now plan on a minimum of a one-third increase in gross each year. In the second year managers were elected in production, sales, and accounting. Called the "M-team," they met with Rachel each week for planning, then followed through on their own, learning what was involved in running a business. By the third year they hired a professional computerized bookkeeper, realizing that the weaving time was the important area to protect.

So the weaver-owners have increasingly taken over the various facets of their business and, other than some designing of new products, consulting on marketing, and acting as advisor to the M-team, Rachel's job now has become primarily the creating of a training curriculum for Tierra Wools. The plan is that after she gives the original courses, those who earn the grade of "Maestra" will teach all future apprentices, working from the manual that she is producing.

In the beginning Rachel and Maria were told by people in the textile world that for the enterprise to be successful, they could not leave the designing to the weavers, and that a "professional" should lay out designs for the weavers to execute. Tierra Wools has proceeded contrary to this advice, however, and encouraged the weavers to get involved in the designing, and this has been built into the curriculum, also. After learning some of the basic principles of design and color, the women are now creating completely personal designs and color schemes. Rachel feels that the result is an exciting indigenous art form.

Every weaving at Tierra Wools is one-of-a-kind. If a *ruana* warp is wound in dark naturals and blacks and this proves to be a popular color, the next warp may be wound with similar colors, but not *exactly* the same. This means that there is progress in design each time, since the weaver is always trying to improve upon her previous piece, and that the skill of the group as a whole is constantly growing.

All of the colors are hand-dyed outdoors, with synthetic dyes in big wash tubs set over pinon and cedar fires. The record dyeing to date was 437 pounds of yarn, done by three artisans in two days. Now they are able to mix their dyes to achieve the exact colors they have in mind for a particular piece of weaving.

In the beginning, when they advertised that they would buy local wool, short-staple contaminated fleeces were offered, and there was bad feeling when they had to turn them down. But now, with Dr. Lyle McNeal as consultant and Antonio Manzanares heading the breeding and wool production program, the Ganados wool growers are producing fine, clean fleeces. Antonio was born and raised in the village. He was a psychology student in college but has returned to his village to raise sheep. As Rachel says, "If you could see the countryside, you would know why; if you knew how difficult it is to make a living here, you would wonder why." Lyle McNeal now directs Utah State University's program for breeding to save the Churro sheep, working with Antonio and other valley farmers.

In the spring of 1986 the original dream became a reality. Tierra Wools bought several hundred pounds of the local "clip" of Columbia-Rambouillet cross, Karakul, and Churro. Some is saved for handspinning, and the rest is sorted and washed and sent to a mill where it is made into yarn to their specification. Now the weavers can say that their yarns and weavings are produced mainly from the fleece grown in the valley. Coarser fleeces are used for rugs, Churro for tapestries, and the fine wool for apparel.

The first Churro fabric became available the following fall; a revival of the traditional *Jerga,* a twill fabric, and *Sabanilla,* a plain-weave or tabby fabric, is in the planning stage. One possibility is to create yardage on fly-shuttle looms for the fashion industry. A marketing trip to New York brought orders, and in their second year Tierra Wools was invited to show in a prestigious Dallas Trade Mart showroom. Neither of these developed into permanent outlets, however. Many of their customers are indeed from New York and Dallas, but the mystique of finding these artisans on a back road of New Mexico in a spectacular setting has proven to be a more high-powered selling technique than the most elegant showrooms. Word has spread and the enchanted customers return.

At first it was thought that they needed to weave some smaller items for local people, instead of catering only to the "rich tourists." But, most popular with customers in the community, as well as tourists, are the more expensive ruanas, rugs, and tapestries. They are pleased to discover that just as in the days when wool and weavings were the mainstay of the economy in this community, most residents realize the value of the work and purchase weavings on lay-away. They are collectors themselves, remembering the days when their mothers and fathers or grandparents were spinners and weavers. They take pride in their community's heritage.

Even though the cooperative structure sometimes threatens to topple the equilibrium of the business and things don't always run smoothly, it is generally realized that this is the only way that they could have done it themselves. An entrepreneur with funds could perhaps have made such a business happen much more easily, but the weavers would then simply be employees. As it is, the weaver-owners will harvest the results of their labor.

Rachel feels that the people involved in Tierra Wools have not only taken giant steps in creating a heritage for their children, fashioned from the best of a two-century-old culture; they have also created a model for creative artisans everywhere who wish to make a decent living with their craft.

The most recent achievement is that they are now able to sort each breed into color lots of 150 pounds, the minimum that a mill will take for spinning. Now Tierra Wools uses all of the wool that is grown in the valley, plus some additional wool that must be purchased because there aren't enough sheep—the opposite of the original situation.

The creation of Tierra Wools has also, I think, been a tremendous accomplishment for Rachel. Her experience with shoestring beginnings for craft enterprises, her utter devotion to the weaving craft, and her ability to share her love of work toward a goal have all been crucial in making Tierra Wools first a believable dream and then a reality.

TOP: *Maria Varela and Molly Manzanares in the weaving workshop.*
BOTTOM: *Kika Chavez at her loom in the old Convent building.*

TOP: *Molly winding a warp and Kika spinning.*
LEFT: *Spring traffic on the main street of Los Ojos.*

LEFT: *San Jose Church, the center of town life.*
BOTTOM: *Angie Serrano dyeing yarns.*

New Horizons

By the spring of 1982 the geographical picture of our family had taken a new turn, and my long relationships with Kristina and Rachel became more officially woven together. Jenny and Rochelle moved back to New Mexico and lived in Talpa, not far from my first home on the ridge above the Ranchos valley. Lorelei and Keith moved west also—towing their belongings in Keith's boat behind his truck—to be married there and start building a house on the El Salto land above Arroyo Seco, where Kinlock, Ian, and Rachel would be their neighbors. Kristina was away in California on a weaving grant at the Gerassi Foundation, so Keith and Lorelei lived in her house while constructing their own. Keith worked with Ian and Kinlock, now experienced builders, learning adobe construction, and thoroughly explored the terrain and wildlife of northern New Mexico. Then when word came to us that Lorelei and Keith were expecting a baby, David, Conor, and I made plans for a winter visit to Taos. This would be Rachel's first grandchild and David's second; his daughter Barbara's son, Sam Postel, was now a year old.

Rachel had the year before made the move to her El Salto land and now lived in a trailer just below Kinlock's house, a lovely spot looking through the tall trees that grew along the acequia below her to the broad expanse of Taos Valley beyond. Her first year there had been rugged. It was a cold winter, the temperature often dropping to twenty below zero. She had no electricity, and having completely lost her sense of smell years before when she was doing silk screen printing without proper ventilation for the chemicals, she was afraid to leave her little gas stove on when she went to sleep. She had to resort to taking her oranges and potatoes into her arctic sleeping bag with her at night to keep them from freezing solid.

In the spring she set up a Navajo loom down in the woods by the stream and in this idyllic setting wove the first foot of a tapestry. Then one day Kristina came to visit and said, "Come on Rachel, let's build you a studio. It won't take any time. I'll help you frame it up." So Rachel set to work digging a foundation and together they started the framing, and it snowed half an inch that night. The framing was finished in three days and then Rachel continued the work with a handsaw and with the help of friends who appeared from time to time. By late fall she was able to move her loom and yarns into the new studio—first onto a dirt floor—and then for Christmas Kristina presented her with a piece of carpeting to lay over the dirt, wall to wall.

It was a year of other beginnings for her too. She started a craft retail cooperative in Taos, and it soon branched off into two co-op shops—Open Space Gallery and Taos Artisans Gallery—which still continue. Jenny was involved in the new Open Space Gallery, as a jeweler. And Rachel and Loraine Mooney set up the Wool Products Association, which would be a point of focus for a number of weaving and spinning ventures in the years to come.

Loraine Mooney had first come to Taos on a camping trip and then took part in a weaving class of Kristina's. She wanted to weave pockets directly into a garment she was weaving, a technique that Kristina wasn't familiar with, so Rachel had come to give a short introduction to that method and Loraine had made a beautiful vest. She decided to return to Taos, and having seen the little house by Kristina's that Ian had built during his spare time from school, asked him to build a house for her—in effect, starting him on his building career. A diligent worker and organizer, she became quietly but effectively involved in many of the spinning and weaving activities in the valley. She would be a charter member of the Mountain and Valley Wool Association and served on the Board of The Inter-Mountain Weavers' Conference as chairman of the Ways and Means Committee for three years. As Kristina said, "Without making any noise at all, she just changed a lot of people's lives."

The Taos Weaving Revival had definitely become an important factor in the creative activity of the valley now. There were many weavers, considerable interest in spinning, and many other new shops were opening. An important figure in this revival was Luisa Gelenter, who with a friend started a spinning and natural dyeing business. Rachel helped them in the beginning and soon they had their own workshop set up. After a few years of this partnership, Luisa continued alone and has become highly skilled in the spinning and blending of natural-dyed yarns, with a beautiful shop, La Lana Wools, in the center of Taos. Luisa's project provided the impetus for the development of a refined version of Rachel and Malcolm's original spinning wheel in 1979. Rachel worked with Bob Easton on the new wheel and then he manufactured them, under the name of Rio Grande Weaver's Supply, until 1985 when she bought the business from him and opened her own retail shop by that name in Taos. She had the wheels produced by Ron Moore, who later also constructed the loom that she designed, as well as other weaving and spinning equipment.

Back East things were also busy. We had finally made the difficult decision to sell the Store in Housatonic, and we moved one of my looms there so I could work while I kept it open in the afternoons with a FOR SALE sign in the window. I took a vacation from tapestries and had a wonderful time weaving simple woolen cloth, spinning white and dark brown wool for it and making pillows for Jenny's new home in Talpa, each pillow a variation of simple brown stripes on lovely soft white wool.

David had, the fall before, completed an exciting architectural project, a greenhouse-pool solar addition to an old New England house. During the winter it had proved very successful, heating the greenhouse and pool, as well as the large house, with about eight cords of wood in the wood-oil furnace that he installed, whereas before the owners had paid exorbitant sums for oil and were never warm. After that we met the young couple who usually house-sat when the owners retreated to a southern island for relief from the New England winter, and they jokingly accused David of ruining their winter schedule. Bougainvillea trailed over the pool from an upper level, and tomatoes ripened in the garden spaces below. Adjoining the greenhouse was a small heat-collecting space, and beyond that a third space for storage of wood for drying under a plastic roof, with open sides for ventilation. David had, over the years, built a number of passive-solar pool-greenhouses, but this was the best test of his theory that even here in the Berkshires solar heating was valid.

Conor had moved downstairs to the studio and to a new stage of independence, and after a summer of carpentry work on David's crew bought his first truck. Kimry and her husband, John, were living in one of our store apartments—Kimry designing and sewing leather bags and John working in a school for disturbed children.

When David, Conor, and I flew out to New Mexico in February, Teresa Rae Loveless was two months old, tiny and blonde, and Rachel a very proud new grandmother. Keith was building their little house, and David and Conor helped to lay the floor; later they planned to build their adobe home next to it, and then Keith would use the first house as a shop. Over dinner in her trailer, Rachel excitedly showed us the beautifully drawn plans she was working on for the house that she hoped to be able to start building soon. It would be a longish rectangle facing the far view south through the trees, and she was already beginning to encourage with irrigation the grass that would be its yard.

Jenny was busy with her jewelry. She was exhibiting in regional shows now and one of her beautiful haircombs of silver intricately inlaid with stones—turquoise, lapis, coral, opal, moss agate, and serpentine—had been purchased by the Albuquerque Museum for their permanent collection. Rochelle was now in school at Mt. Wheeler Nursery. All of the family and friends gathered at Jenny's for Lorelei and Ian's joint birthday party with a grand Spanish feast. Keith, David, and Conor made expeditions into the countryside and climbed San Antonio Mountain in the snow to look for elk. It was a fine visit and we were reluctant to leave. Conor would graduate in June and was already making plans to return to Taos as soon as possible. Back in Massachusetts, it seemed quite natural that we began to think of finding a small piece of land in New Mexico where we could build a little cabin to stay in when we went west.

While in New Mexico I had arranged to show my work at the Mission Gallery in Taos and also had several shows planned in the New England area. When the store building finally sold, I began weaving at home again. David was busy with another greenhouse addition and Conor with school, and during his spring vacation we drove south to meet the family on Florida's Big Pine Key where Keith, Lorelei, and little Teresa were living in their camper, Keith enjoying a winter as a commercial fisherman. Ian, Kinlock, and various friends came for shorter periods, and while we were there Rachel also came for a few weeks. While the fishermen were out at sea, Rachel and I, in our tent, began reminiscing on tape about the "old days" of beginning to weave in Taos. Her stop at Big Pine Key was on a roundabout route to New York, where she was taking several suitcases of weavings from Tierra Wools, hoping to set up outlets for them there.

Winter seemed to linger longer than usual that year, especially after our stay in the south. Immense flocks of geese were still flying over on their way north after we returned, and at the sound of their honking we would dash outdoors to watch them. This vast event, with sometimes hundreds of birds in a flock moving as one for such great distances, was an awe-inspiring mystery to me. They stayed in my mind and I came to see them as an image of history, of evolution—a magnificent display of cumulative experience, of all the past distilled in the present. It was like incredibly beautiful sky writing—a message written large in the sky, moving toward some goal, as if they were calling out in their wonderfully raucous voices to attract us as witnesses to the spectacle of their success as a species. Perhaps, also, the migrations of our family kept their image in my mind.

After graduation Conor worked as a carpenter for the summer, and then in August he did return to Taos to work for Ian and Keith, living in an apartment in town near Jenny and Rochelle's new home. David and I flew out for Christmas and stayed in various borrowed houses, including the first, newly built room of Rachel's while she was away conducting a spinning workshop. That was the first of what was to become the pattern of Christmas mornings, moving from presents and breakfast at one family house to another. Conor and Kinlock had created wonderful presents, photographs that Conor had taken from Kinlock's airplane of each family's home—Jenny's a wonderful view of the town of Taos from the air, Malcolm's with him standing in front of his house stark naked, waving his arms wildly in greeting.

That year we went to the Taos Pueblo for Christmas Eve where traditionally, after everything is in readiness at home for the following morning, everyone goes for the procession. It was the first time in many years for me, the first for Conor since he was an infant, and a new experience for David. Just as darkness was descending over the Sacred Mountain people began to gather in the broad plaza between the two great pueblos. Bells rang in the tower of the little white-painted adobe church in the plaza and Indians, some in blankets, some in everyday dress, quietly crossed through the crowd to the church for Mass. From outside we caught glimpses of the brightly candle-lit and colorful interior where the almost full-sized figure of the Virgin, dressed in white satin and wearing a crown, stood by the altar.

There were *faralitos* set up alongside the path that the procession would take around the plaza—very pitchy split pieces of wood arranged in towers—and as we moved around to keep our circulation working in the cold, Indians lit a few of them and great clouds of the blackest smoke poured up into the night sky, sending up wild orange flames and showering us with sparks. The magic of Christmas in Taos had begun and finally the tower bell of the church tolled again, spreading its sound through the night in the lovely way that I remembered over so many years in the valley. Then the old men with the drums drew the procession from the church, chanting, singing, proceeding slowly along the path between the by now wildly burning faralitos. There was the sound of the drums, the billowing smoke, the bright flames, and the Virgin carried on a platform under her white canopy, followed by singing women and a group of tiny children, brightly dressed, giggling and dancing in a little pattern.

Slowly they proceeded around the plaza, the crowd following. It was a great swirling phenomenon of light and dark: firelight, illuminated faces, Indians, strangers, friends; Rochelle and her Uncle Conor hand in hand; groups of blanketed Indians appearing and disappearing against the backdrop of the great earthen pueblo; the large winter night, then the sound of guns that surprisingly periodically accompanied the procession. After a while at the Pueblo one becomes tuned to a different kind of time, begins to feel the space, feel the silent footsteps on the ancient earth, feel the presence of the mountain that has retreated into the darkness above. The silent graciousness with which the Indians allow the visitors to become in some way a part of their ancient ceremonies, on this night blended with the only centuries-old ceremony of Christmas, always affects us there. When the procession was over we wandered to our cars, looking back into the darkness where little groups of people still stood silhouetted against the brilliant flames of the fires that were still burning, with a sense of having very simply but powerfully participated in a blending of earth and sky and fire and humanity.

Des Montes Again

For our last two weeks we moved to Ian's little adobe cabin across the yard from Kristina's house, the one he had built years before, during a summer between college years—a tiny three-room building that incorporated, in miniature, many of the charming facets of adobe construction. An adobe half-wall made shelves for the minimal kitchen on one side and a corner for a little raised fireplace in the living room on the other; then above everything there was a small sleeping loft, reached by a ladder, with a window for enjoying the desert view.

Kristina's establishment had grown again. Now she had a separate weaving studio—a generous space filled with looms and festooned with dozens of hanks of yarn in the bright colors she loved—and attached behind that she had also built a wood shop. In the weaving room two large and one small loom were set up, and on two of these she continued to weave her, by now, "traditional" rugs and blankets of heavy, brightly dyed yarns. On the third loom she was embarking on new adventures, in the "playing around" stage of a completely new sort of tapestry. She was beginning to weave the bright allegorical-figured pieces that would absorb her for the next few years. She wove simple and dramatic figures of people and animals—often playful and humorous—and juxtaposed in surprising ways on simple grounds of white or single colors. They were delightful and provocative, and she was excited at finding this truly personal tapestry form and pleased with our response to them.

One day she took us out across the gorge to Tres Piedras to see the Rio Grande Wool Mill in which she was very much involved. That project had begun back in 1978. Bob Richardson had been a prime mover in getting the Wool Products Association started, an organization that was to be the focus for using local

147

resources—sheep, spinners, and weavers—and trying to get grant money for developing these. This activity was to begin around John Ussery's carding machine. John's great enthusiasm and talent was for inventing machinery and methods for working with wool and the production of yarn, and he had gotten a grant for building a scouring mill to clean the wool.

The association had hired Rachel as a consultant to work up a proposal for this development of a wool industry in northern New Mexico. She recommended that they proceed in several phases, the first to move John's carding machine down the mountain to a location where it would be more generally accessible. She had been driving up into the mountains on an often almost impassable road, lurching over boulders and straddling washouts, to work on the wool batts that they were producing together and knew that it was not a site for a growing wool industry.

The second phase would be the setting up of John's scouring plant at the new location for cleaning the local wool. The third would be the dyeing of the wool for the carded blends that she was designing; the fourth, to market the carded wool. This would actually be an expansion of the small business that she had already begun. She had been washing and dyeing wool, going up the mountain to card the colored wool blends, then spinning the wool herself and selling it under her own label. David and I had carried these lovely skeins of homespun—soft blends and rich, bold ones— in our store back in Housatonic.

They heard that Lorraine Trujillo and her father, who ran about five thousand sheep, were getting a wool mill, and the new plan was to have this new mill custom spin a few lines of yarn that they would market. Then, if all went well, the association could try to set up its own centrally located mill. There was some difference of opinion as to whether the proper role of WPA was simply as a vehicle for exchange of ideas and mutual support or whether it should become a commercial venture. So a two-day meeting was set up at Ghost Ranch, near Abiquiu, for the working out of a general plan.

One of the first accomplishments of the meeting was the re-naming of the organization as the Mountain and Valley Wool Association or MAVWA, the name proposed by Maria Varela, with whom Rachel had worked in setting up Tierra Wools. They were pleased with the actual "mountain and valley" shapes of the letters in MAVWA. Then John dramatically announced that he had located a wool mill for sale in New Hampshire that was very cheap, only about four thousand dollars. Kristina was not at that time a member of the association but had heard of the new ideas afoot and came to the meeting. She recalls that the reaction to John's statement had been surprisingly slight and the subject was soon dropped, but she tossed and turned in excitement all night afterward; and at the next day's meeting, in spite of Rachel's urging her to "wait and see," she volunteered to put up some seed money if others would also. Rachel and Kristina drove home together and, fired with excitement, stopped along the way to look at several possible empty buildings. Then the next day Kristina remembered the large, pink adobe schoolhouse in Tres Piedras, which had for some years been unused except by the owner's cows in bad weather. After some negotiation that became the future home of the Rio Grande Wool Mill.

Transporting the large and extremely heavy machinery of the mill from New Hampshire was quite an enterprise. While John was off on that mission, Ian and Seth undertook the heroic job of preparing the site for it. They cut a huge door in the side of the building, removed two floors to create a space that was 120 feet long and two stories high, then brought Seth's tractor inside and spread dozens of loads of gravel over the dirt floor. Also the badly leaking roof had to be repaired and half of the windows replaced.

Then the mill arrived—a huge flatbed truck loaded with a series of long, mysterious, and extremely heavy machines. The real challenge was to safely transfer it all from the truck to its resting place inside. Seth and Ian had arranged for the REA hoist to be on hand—the biggest crane in northern New Mexico—and somehow the job was accomplished successfully, with neither machines nor people damaged. The truck driver pronounced it the best job of difficult unloading he had ever seen, especially by inexperienced hands.

There were many more hurdles, though, before this incredible intricacy of machinery could be expected to produce yarns of the sizes and sorts needed. The proper conditions of humidity had to be accomplished and the machinery, which had been used back in New England for spinning fine suiting yards, had to be adjusted to produce the heavier yarns that they wanted. Though their eventual aim was to use only northern New Mexico sheep's wool, in the beginning they had huge bales of wool shipped from Texas.

Kristina served on the board of directors, and was also very emotionally involved in the success of the project, intrigued with its potentialities, with finding solutions to its problems. There was considerable changeover, both of production and business staff, over the next several years, but through many ups and downs there was forward progress and fine yarn was produced. A local man, Harold Montoya, was initiated by John into the mysteries of working with wool and the machinery of spinning and stayed with the mill throughout its operation.

Kristina showed us through the mill, from the room where the wool was sorted and put through a picker for loosening, to pass through a chute that carried it down to the vast spinning room. There it passed from machine to machine, to be gradually carded into a smooth web, and finally to emerge as strands called "tapes" which were then combined and spun into 2-tape, 3-tape, or 5-tape yarns. The mill produced mostly white yarn but also made some blends of lovely pearl-grays and some darker mixtures. I collected a supply of these yarns to work with back in Massachusetts.

Rachel's Tierra Wools in Los Ojos was by this time under way, and her project became an important source of business for the mill, both establishments benefiting from the concidence of timing. For her Rio Grande Weaver's Supply, Rachel also used the mill's yarn, dyeing it into the beautiful array of colors that she was developing for her store. One of her special talents was creating an inspiring arrangement of materials; one whole wall in the shop was now filled with shelves of these colored yarns, and she had space to hang her tapestries as well. Large baskets of carded wool and mohair for spinning filled another side of the room—luscious natural colors and blends—along with the looms that she was producing.

Later, the larger shop next door became available and she rented that and, joining the spaces with a large doorway, opened Weaving Southwest—a gallery of tapestries, rugs, and other woven items, realizing a long-dreamed-of plan much sooner than she had expected. This was a landmark move, the first setting for specifically exhibiting tapestries in the valley, and it became an important focus for weavers in the area, even beyond Taos. It was wonderful to see our work well displayed on the walls there, along with handsome rugs and rows of pillows. At first she also showed handwoven apparel, thinking that this would sell more readily and more or less support the display of tapestries, but to her surprise, the greatest response was to the tapestries. There were other craft shops now with fine apparel collections, such as Open Space Gallery, so she began showing only rugs and pillows along with the wall hangings.

In the very last week of our stay we fund our piece of land— 2.3 acres near Arroyo Seco in the area called Des Montes where I had lived many years before—which satisfied our primary requirement of an open view of the desert to the west and was not far from most of our family. The plan was to build not only a house for us, but also one for Jenny and Rochelle near the front of the land, and before we left David began to work on plans with Jenny for her house, which would be built first, in readiness for Keith and Ian to begin construction when they had time from other jobs.

On the last day, we took a full-circle panoramic series of photos from the center of the land so that we could absorb our new environment back in the East. It was even harder to leave now, but David had several design projects waiting for him, not to mention work that had to be done on our own house so that it could be rented when we were able to get away. We had also started to think in terms of eventually making a permanent move. Then in April another grandson was born, Barbara's son, Rafael Postel.

Conor returned also and for him a busy year ensued, working on carpentry jobs and with a sculptress friend, Annie Basse, on building playgrounds. He had begun to work with stone as well as wood and had a wonderful feel for this material, which he loved. He and David faced the new terraces of our yard with stone, and then Conor built a beautiful stone wall at the entrance to our drive, the stones so well selected that they appeared to have been carved to fit together. He even managed to include a trip to Florida between jobs, as well as driving a friend out to school in Colorado, with a few days spent in Taos on the way back.

David's new design project was an exciting one, a large house and guest house with a solar-heated pool enclosed between them, which he was also building. But when word came from New Mexico in July that Keith and Ian would soon be free to begin building Jenny's house he managed to leave the work in progress and we made a whirlwind trip out to consult, and especially to plan exactly where her house, and eventually ours, would sit on the land. We took pictures with family members standing on what would be the corners of each house so that from back home we could try to imagine the structures that would soon begin to happen there. Except for wild rose and plum bushes along the irrigation ditch at the front of the land, there was nothing larger than sage and chamisa growing; but we were already forming close ties with our two acres and imagining where we would plant our orchard and start our garden.

Exciting pictures started arriving in our mail, of Rochelle standing beside the first few courses of adobe bricks that would become the walls of her room, then of the whole structure of rooms ready for the pouring of the bond beam on which the roof would rest. And finally there came indoor pictures of a plastering party—with Rochelle's father, Pepe, and other family members—smoothing mud over the archway that led from the living room into the solar hallway where Jenny's plants would soon stand. In October we celebrated Conor's twentieth birthday and toasted Jenny and Rochelle in their new home and the news that Lorelei and Keith would be having another child in the spring.

We celebrated Christmas in Massachusetts, as it turned out for the last time, and in January drove west, hurled by a violent snowstorm across western New York State, arriving in high spirits at Jenny's door. Her house was beautiful and looked very settled with plants by the windows, Oli's paintings and my tapestries on the walls; in her kitchen was the round New Mexican table that had moved with my household ever since we acquired and refinished it in the first Des Montes house across the fields on the Valdez rim.

There were big plans afoot for a family fishing trip to the tip of Baja California. I was content to stay with Jenny and Rochelle, but David and Conor would go with the caravan that included Malcolm, Seth, Kinlock, Ian—and of course the prime mover, Keith, who would tow his boat, T-Rae. It turned out to be a trip of almost mythical proportions with adventures all along the way, grand ocean fishing, camping on beaches and exploring the terrain in detail. When Rachel, Lorelei, Teresa, and Suzanne, Ian's girl-friend, flew down for several weeks midway through the stay, the men had found a grand, semi-finished house to rent on the beach near Cabo and everyone moved indoors. Conor loved it and caught his share of giant fish. The stories of adventure began to echo back to New Mexico even before the travelers returned, and when they did, there were many sessions of looking at slides and photos, and telling of stories, to each other and to Kristina, Jenny, Rochelle, and me, the only family members who weren't there.

Back in Des Montes I had borrowed Rachel's typewriter and happily put in long days of work, periodically taking breaks to wander over the sage meadows out behind our land and musing over the spot where our house, or at least the beginning of it, would perhaps stand by the end of the year. Our plans were under way, the house to be a wide U, enclosing a greenhouse and pool, where the solar heated water would be stored, heat the house, and provide year-round exercise. But first only two rooms and a bath would be built, which, if our hopes were realized, would be ready for us by the following Christmas.

Conor

Conor stayed on in Taos for the rest of the winter; he worked on Kinlock's building crew, went skiing, and also taught Rochelle to ski. Keith soon had our walls started, and when Conor hitchhiked home to Housatonic in May, he reported that he had actually walked on the tile floors of our new home. We had news for him, too: Keith and Lorelei's son, Tyler Campbell Loveless, had just been born. Then Conor had a wonderful idea. If we were really moving west for good he thought that Rochelle should come east for one last visit with us there in the house she had known since she was little. We agreed that it was a brilliant idea and soon it was arranged; she would arrive by plane on July 2 and be with us for two weeks.

It was a wonderful visit. We four and a friend of Conor's went down to New York—Rochelle's first train ride—for the anniversary celebration of the Statue of Liberty and the Tall Ships festivities. We visited Oli in his studio and saw his beautiful bright new paintings and all had lunch together in Chinatown. Then Conor and his friend went their way and David, Rochelle, and I braved the crowds and viewed the masses of boats and people around the downtown docks and showed Rochelle the city— uptown and downtown, by subway and bus and yellow cab.

We stayed with our friend Ruth Bronz in her tiny apartment next door to her new restaurant, Miss Ruby's Cafe. Ruth was an old and dear friend who had lived near us in Housatonic, with whom we had shared many traditions before she moved her restaurant from West Stockbridge to the city: wonderful many-coursed Thanksgiving feasts at her house, July 4 barbecues at our land, fishing the herring runs in May followed by pickling and canning of the silvery fish late into the night, and countless evenings of delicious talk. She was one of the people we would greatly miss when we moved west. Rochelle was impressed with the city sounds, now punctuated with the explosions of firecrackers, that came in our open window at night. With Ruth and Michael Dorsey we watched the procession of Tall Ships with friends from their eleventh-floor apartment overlooking the river, a grand sight. Then we took the train home, following the Hudson River north into craggy, tree-covered country again.

On the evening before my birthday, Conor and several friends invited Rochelle to join them for a movie, and the next morning I discovered that they had actually spent the evening collecting masses of flowers; on the kitchen table was a glorious, vast canning tub full of them waiting for me—dozens of varieties of blooms.

The weekend before she left we joined a barn-raising party for our and Conor's old friends, Kate and Joel DeGaramo. As the day progressed the posts and then the beams rose, up two stories on an old stone barn foundation—with Conor pounding home pegs in the joints and then dashing off into the woods to bring back a roof tree, which was triumphantly nailed to the final peak of the roof. It was a grand and dramatic day to wind up Rochelle's visit, and she flew home again.

Just two weeks later an unimaginable family tragedy struck. We lost our beloved Conor in an automobile accident, on July 30, 1986. Jenny and Rochelle, Keith and his family and Kristina came from New Mexico, Oli and Ruth and Michael from New York, Barb from Detroit, Kimry and John and Amy and Conor's many friends, all came—and together we have somehow gotten from that point to this.

His friends were marvelously loving and supportive. Some of them came by, and we sent with them the message that they were all welcome. That evening a dozen or so young people appeared and we visited; they were very sweet, telling us Conor stories and looking at pictures of the great Baja California trip the family took that past winter, which was such a great event for him. Then they asked if they could go down to Conor's room for a while, and did. We realized that more people had joined them, and periodically little groups would wander up and talk, then go downstairs again.

His room had been sort of a gathering place for them. When I had straightened it up I had put there a big bouquet of flowers from our garden—and had left things as he had—his leather tool belt on the table where he had dropped it after work. His favorite special shirt was a bright-colored handwoven Guatemalan one that Jenny had given me and he had adopted; it was a kind of symbol of something and I had, I suppose, for that reason dropped it on the bed.

The evening wore on with this roving visiting up and down-stairs, and finally David told them it was getting late and suggested that we all go down together for a while. We all did—the whole family was still there. It was an amazing experience—twenty or so kids, just being there, listening to music quietly. In one corner they had made a sort of altar; they had put the bouquet there and beside it his cowboy boots—and beside them was the shirt in a heap. The light was low and we all sat or stood around the edges of the room. They had straightened the old straw hat on the buck's head on the wall and put a white plastic lei around its neck.

The kids went ahead with the ineffable kind of ceremony that was happening—they just moved around the room, occasionally hugging, crying a little, stopping to leaf through the pictures that lay on the table, talking little. As I watched, I had the feeling that they moved around separately together—and that together they were holding something up—all intent on loving Conor. A friend, later when I told her about it, said, "It was Conor's spirit they were holding up." I went over with them by the little altar, looking at the pictures, and when I cried they held me in their arms and then wandered around again, without words and totally without pretense. At one point, six or so of us began to dance for a few moments, as Conor would have been doing.

Finally we said it was time to go and one of the boys, Gabe, said, "There's one more thing to do." He then passed out beers while someone worked to find a certain song on the Beatles tape they were playing. He gathered everyone close together, kids and family and all, and they played "Here Comes the Sun," which they said was Conor's song—and we hugged and loved Conor—and when it was over they filed out, each giving us one last hug. Then each car tooted goodbye as they drove out.

Later, Keith told us that he had been walking the baby out in the yard and saw the kids through the glass doors, one after the other putting on the Guatemalan shirt and passing it to the next.

Someone told our pastor about that evening, and at the service at the church he ended his talk with "Here comes the sun."

❿ ❿ ❿

For a year and a half the only writing that I did was in what I came to call my Conor Folio—my survival journal. Through it I found some small comforts. I realized that we don't use up past experiences—even those from long ago; we can continue to experience them, can almost say they still exist, are still going on. Any little experience—looking at a flower—we experience more than we consciously recognize, and we can look back and sense more of how it was. It seems that our present is always a blending of things we have been or felt or seen with what we are encountering now. And with each new present we use some selected bits of the past, too.

David, Conor, and I were so close for so many years that it took us a year or so to be able to enjoy vacations without him when he began, as he grew up, to want to go off on his own with his friends. For a while we both felt a little foolish when we realized that we regretted seeing special things because Conor wasn't seeing them with us. Of course we outgrew that gradually and could enjoy ourselves—but he *was* fun to have along.

Now we learned from his friends that they had experienced this, too. I tried to figure out how it was that he communicated with people. It seemed that he expressed something special that was more or less intangible, but very much felt. There was a kind of intensity of feeling that he seemed to edge things with—not exactly toward people, but more *with* people. He seemed to be saying, "This is really great, this is really important. *We* are really great, there's really great stuff here." He communicated passion. He seemed to communicate that there was more that we were searching for—that we had to look for what else was there.

One of his friends said, "When people were sort of down he would make them laugh, would pick up a *stone* or something and somehow make a big thing of it and make everybody feel better." We also learned that he had close friends of all ages, that with him people were totally unconscious of his or their age. He simply loved people and made them feel valuable.

One day we received a letter from a woman whom we didn't

know, which said, "Conor came to build stone walls at my house last summer and he soon saw all sorts of ways in which he could enhance the look of the place. And one day he led me into the garden to show me his surprise—a stone throne made of lintel stones found in the woods, where one could sit and look out over the phlox garden. He smiled so, to see the delight on my face. . . . So that is now Conor's throne, where something of his rare and touching spirit will surely linger."

On October 11, his twenty-first birthday, we and many of his friends gathered at the top of our land beside the immense gray stone that rose from the rocky mountainside where we had first planned to build our house, to carve a monument for him. Our friend Annie Basse brought her sculpture tools and showed people how to use them and after the letters were stenciled with chalk we all worked through the day and carved C O N O R in an arc of large letters across the stone, then the date, and above it all a rising sun, which his friends said was his symbol.

Around the base of the rock we planted daffodil bulbs and now, every spring, David's daughter Amy sends us a picture of their new blooming. And every October some of his friends go there to camp for the night as they did that night after David and I walked back down the hill.

Home at Last

It seems that it is easier to project a sort of generalized goal than it is to, later, really comprehend that this dearly held goal has been reached. It surprises me that I am so calm about finally being in New Mexico for good, for all the year round. For so long it seemed a major miracle yet to be accomplished; now, finally, it is actual fact and we are too busy to be amazed. Often, though, in the midst of the busyness, I am struck with the reality of what has happened—with this house that surrounds me, with the adobe of the walls, the scene out one or another window—scenes that have appeared to me more often, perhaps, in memory than reality over these years; and I am amazed at the texture of reality, at the similarity between the imagined this and actually being here.

Changes in the valley have continued, of course. What was, earlier, empty farm or sagebrush land along the road north from Taos has been developed in many areas and looks quite different from the period, long ago, when I drove along it to my home on the rim above Valdez. The main highway from Taos south to Ranchos de Taos has become a commercial strip, accommodating the needs of the growing population in the valley and the tourist industry that is important to its economic welfare. The number of galleries is astounding; new home construction appears to be continuous. But in the country, away from all of this activity, the *feel* of the place is the same. The mountains and the desert are still there, the setting is still rural, our view peaceful.

Now the presentiment of fall is in the air. I sit out on the portal and gaze wonderingly to the north—out over our land and the fields and pasture beyond to the intermittent line of trees that mark the ridge over Valdez Valley, and across it to Lobo's mountain. My eyes travel over the complexities of its folds, its triangular structure—first dotted with pinons, then up to where the heights are less steep slopes of softer green, great swaths of aspen groves in which I have never walked. Over the years that I have lived here I've never explored that section of the mountains. The lower western end I know a little; that's where the Hawk Ranch lies, and I've wandered up its canyons by the small, richly green-edged streams, under the great ponderosas, below the hanging cliffs of rock. And I've hiked on the highest peaks off to the east—even the bald slopes of Wheeler Peak, the highest of all—far back so that it is visible from only a few points in the valley. Over all the years that Lobo's mountain has been the backdrop for my life, my connection with it has been largely visual.

Now finally, though, we occasionally go on sorties up onto the lower slopes, into the complex ridges and canyons where rough road tracks have been scraped for one reason or another—to old short-lived mines, to an abandoned reclusive homestead clinging to the hillside and beginning to be camouflaged with fallen brush and pine needles. On the lowest slopes the roads are more carefully carved, leading to new homesites that now are sprinkled above Valdez Valley. Beyond these there is a feeling of being in another world, another atmosphere. It is simpler; the elements of which it is all made can be counted, it seems—just trees and rocks and dirt, it appears at first. Then small dry tufts of several grasses come into focus, then clumps of flowers, small pincushions of cactus here and there, a flash of blue from a mountain jay chattering in a clump of oaks, a small lizard, but overall it is a sparse place. At a certain altitude the air becomes different; it feels high and distilled, has a different pulse, a different sound, the sound of air moving through pine needles. Then higher up, where David and Keith go on horseback, it is deep mountain forest.

One of the taller clumps of trees in the line that denotes the ridge over Valdez is the one that shades the house where I lived many years ago, where I began weaving tapestries. It was from there that I got to know those mountains visually. They were the place from which I knew the deer came down to the valley floor to browse amongst the farms in the winter after a snowfall, their tracks intertwining with those of the cows. The valley set the mountain apart in a particular way. It was a place to look for the beginning of changes in the seasons. One day there would be an indefinable but clear difference in the look of the air, even on a clear day, and I would watch it to see what might be about to happen. It might only be a day's storm in which great pieces of the mountain would become veiled shapes of huge crouched animals or would disappear altogether. As a day passed, it was sometimes as though the mountain was being created, drawn or painted or sculpted as you watched, a ridge built up there or a valley shaped out of evening shadows, made by them on the spot, for the first time. It was impossible to say exactly what the mountain was because it was thus constantly being re-created, constantly happening and only very, very faintly understood.

From the other side of our house—the sunny, southern side— I can look across a few fields to where Kristina lives. Of the three of us she is the only one who has stayed put. We and Rochelle sometimes walk there, turning off our road to follow a smaller dirt one, narrow and edged with wild plums, then cutting through the edges of some fields and over some fences to her pasture, where the llamas stop their grazing to watch us. Their small barn and corrals are just beyond the pond that she and Seth made a few years ago to water first her pastures and then his, tucked close to thickets of plum and willow that have grown high along the web of irrigation ditches that interlaces her property.

The small rectangle that was her home when I first went there has grown in every possible direction. Every time we returned its shape had changed. A patio had been added, then it had turned into a room and some bits of wall had enclosed another outdoor space. Then when she built her weaving room and shop a little apart, the rough ground between them gradually became grassy yard. The ditch that meandered from the farther main ditch fed Russian olive and plum trees in the yard, and they grew surprisingly tall and flower beds interspersed with vegetable patches appeared. The ditch finally was lined with stone and became a small canal with two little plank bridges crossing it, leading to her front and back doors, and lilacs and apple trees grew bouffant along it. The house grew again, a wall reaching almost to the ditch, and a little bedroom appeared above the kitchen from which she could look out over the trees and see the far view. Now we sit in a patio that is shaded by a tall elm and remember when we had picnics there, roasting corn in a fireplace we had just constructed beside a little elm she had just planted, wondering if one day it would be tall enough to hold a swing for our grandchildren. So Kristina's house has not only been her home, but is also for me a visible chronicle of all the years and all the changes that have happened for all of us.

Rachel's home, like mine, has moved here and there over the valley and sometimes out of it, though not so far or for so long, and now she, too, is settled with children and grandchildren just a yard away. Her house is elegantly simple, a long rectangle that steps slightly down the land, with tall windows facing her yard and flowers and the grand view to the south. Her original room, the kitchen, is long and spacious and some of our large family dinner gatherings now take place there.

On most Thursdays, even through the winter, she and her assistant, Ann Houston, spend the day outside in front of the little weaving studio dyeing up huge batches of yarn for her shop. They constructed a firebrick fire pit, which is covered with a cast iron top with circular openings to hold the two large dyeing tubs; over that is a system of two pulleys that hold and lift five pounds of wet yarn into and out of the pots. The dyed yarns are finally rinsed indoors in her washing machine, the skeins straightened, and by afternoon the deck outside her door has bloomed with rows of colored yarns drying in the sun.

It seems that the collective windows of all of our houses together accomplish the framing of all of the facets of what is most special, visually, about this valley. One of the things that is best seen from Rachel's windows is the view far to the south of the canyon of the Rio Grande where its walls appear to be a series of steps before it drops down at the foot of the Picuris Mountains to enter the valley on the way to Santa Fe, distant enough to often be veiled in shades of gray-blue.

Ian and Seth traded pieces of land, and now on our way to Kristina's we pass the acres of apricot orchard that Seth planted from seeds some years back and the simple, beautiful house he constructed by the ancient method of puddled adobe; and Ian has built on the El Salto family land. Keith and Lorelei's house, with a pitched tin roof of the style most typical of the New Mexico mountain villages where the snowfall is greatest, has also the feel of a New England adobe. Above them the fields of El Salto continue to rise, step by step until the foothills give way to the craggy cliffs of El Cuchillo and the mountains beyond.

We spent our first Christmas without Conor in the two rooms that Keith had built for us on our land, in the midst of family. We drove out from Massachusetts in our truck, heavily loaded with treasured belongings—my piano first, and then at the very back of the load three sizable lilac bushes, given to me one birthday by Kimry, Jenny, and Conor, which David had dug up at the last moment and lashed on. Our black cat, Catapetl, also came with us, hiding for most of the trip behind our seat. The house actually sat there, just as we had seen in photos, and the family was there to help us unload. Soon these new spaces, just two rooms, were very full of familiar things. Kristina had made a surprise for us, a lovely small adobe fireplace in the corner of the living room, as a housewarming present and soon we had a fire going. Now we could really envision the rest of the house beyond the kitchen and living room doors. While we were there Jenny helped us apply in the living room the color coat of *tierra bayita,* grayish-white earth that we dug from the bank of an arroyo in Llano Quemado, beyond Ranchos, mixed with some sand, some fine flakes of mica, and flour to give it firmness; and when we had cleaned up after this rather messy procedure, the effect was truly grand, set off by the floor of square Mexican tiles. In this setting we worked out many details of our plans and also watched the excavation of the swimming pool hole, now outside, in what would be the greenhouse room.

After two months we flew back East and finished up work that had to be done, sold our house and land there to people who seemed ready to treasure them, and made the final move—all in something of a haze with the pulls of past, present, and future—and with plans for visits by Kimry, John, and Amy soon in the new home in the West.

Keith and his crew had begun the walls for the rest of the house when we returned in June, and David joined his crew. With what seemed miraculous speed, Keith had the stacks of adobe bricks transformed into rooms, the pool constructed and filled with water, the beams swung into place by a gigantic crane dramatic against the blue sky, then finally roofed over. Last came the earth plastering of the walls and the laying of tiles, and David and I hacked small *nichos* into the wall adobes of the hall that ran along the side of the greenhouse, leading to the studio and bed-rooms. Above this hallway was a long series of slanting glass panes that threw sunlight onto the high bank of plastic tubing through which the pool's water would pass periodically, to be heated and returned to the pool, from where its heat warmed the house. This was the crux of David's solar heating system, his theory that it should serve several purposes, aesthetic as well as practical. These windows would also give us a view of the stars at night and of the changing weather. The many plants that we had brought with us now sat in pots on the earth that would become the greenhouse, already enjoying the sun that poured in through windows all along the south wall. Among them were palms and key limes and papayas that we had grown from seeds collected on our trip to Big Pine Key a few years before.

Living was rather chaotic in the midst of this construction, but the chaos gradually lessened and by August we were able to spread out the furniture that had been packed into two rooms, retrieve the things that had been stored in Keith's barn, and have a grand cleaning for a small family reunion—David's sister, brother, and cousin and some of their family—with a housewarming party for crew and neighbors along with the family.

Only then did we realize the grand success of David's design. The greenhouse-pool room was long and dramatic and, sur-rounding it, the living rooms each became comfortably centered with their particular functions. David lined one wall of the tiny study with bookshelves, and that became my work room as well as a guest room, an inward-facing space with just one small win-dow to the north and the view of Lobo Peak. The studio, on the west, was spacious and filled with light, and in it stood David's drawing table and my loom and cabinets filled with our working materials. In our room, next to it, David built his first adobe fireplace, and there the windows faced the desert, where we could see the sun first fall on the far horizon as it cleared the peaks behind us in the early mornings.

Our belongings looked very much at home—the old chestnut table David had made for our first home, old handmade pieces we had acquired with our store in Housatonic, pictures and tap-estries on the walls, our books. It was surprising how perfectly and cozily all of these elements fitted together and became our New Mexico home.

Our land slanted slightly down to the west, and we had set the house *into* this slope to keep a lower profile; and Keith had laid in the foundation for a patio wall on that east side, toward the mountains, when he made the house foundations. Now we built those walls, made flower beds beside the house, paved the area just outside the kitchen, and then David and Rochelle raked and seeded with grass the rest of the patio within the wall for the spring sprouting of a lawn.

It was such a delight to have Rochelle right next door, popping in every now and then to see if something interesting was going on and always ready for a walk or an expedition. She was becoming much involved in dance classes and now took part in productions at the Taos Community Auditorium, happily going to what seemed to us endless rehearsals. She liked to be busy.

It was a lovely September. The birds were flocking, part of the slightly changed atmosphere that meant fall was beginning to happen. Blackbirds moved in a group pattern from field to field, to fence, to telephone line, feeding on the seeds that were now dry and falling, seeming to be tuning in to each other and to the group pattern that would be their identity when they moved out of familiar surroundings. It was all such a mystery, involving things so out of our ken, and so beautiful to see them move in the air as with one mind, making a form in space in which the parts worked together but never touched. They seemed to me to be excited about what lay ahead.

The nights were a little chillier, and the days, though sunny and warm, were no longer hot. Then gold and yellow began to appear over the valley. We watched the turning of the aspens on the mountains; first only a warm hint of color, then whole streaks and patches of gold. It had been many years since I had watched this happen. Twice we had been here in the fall, on our first trip out with Jenny and Conor when they were sixteen and six and then for Rochelle's birth, but we left before the turning of the leaves the first time and came after it was accomplished, the second.

In early October there was a happy family wedding. Ian Wilson and Suzanne Wiggin were married in the lovely old adobe church in Arroyo Hondo, and then everyone gathered in Kristina's yard for feasting and dancing through the afternoon.

Then on October 11 family and friends gathered with us and we planted a Conor Garden of all kinds of bulbs that would bloom for our next spring—in the shape of a large C, beside the path to Jenny's house. Once when he was in his early teens and we with difficulty had prevailed upon him to interrupt his activities with his regular job of mowing the grass, we looked down from the house after a while to see that the lawn was not only mowed, but autographed. He had mowed everything neatly except for ten-foot letters spelling C O N O R, across the whole lower yard!

It was good to know that we were finally home. When I had lived in New Mexico before, though I felt at home I knew that being here was not permanent. Now my whole system was learning, very slowly, to calm down, knowing that I was finally really home. From earliest childhood, home for me was a moveable feast. Moving was simply what families did periodically; they packed all their treasures and embarked on another adventure in location. There was always the assumption in my mind at the time that the move under way would prove to be to our *real home*—though, at my childhood's end I discovered that Home was a composite image of a number of homes, selected because of certain qualities that they shared from an even larger group of places actually lived in. Sometimes now, I feel that those "certain qualities" have all finally come together to form one image.

Certainly this home, this house and its environs, is beautiful. The house is a real creation of our imaginations, designed to fit our needs, and we are often startled at the structure we have projected. We have set the scene and now we must continue with the living, lay out the details in the framework of time.

Going Ahead

Kimry and John came out for the first Christmas in our full-fledged new home. After the festivities at the Pueblo we all went to Kristina's for supper and skating on her pond by the light of a great bonfire, a yearly party attended by many more than family. Then in the morning we walked next door through the snow for Jenny's traditional Christmas breakfast with freshly baked Finnish *pulla* from her grandmother's recipe and the opening of presents.

We carried over Amy's heavy box that had just arrived from Massachusetts and in the bottom, under her jams and relishes and gingerbreads and stollen, found a truly wonderful surprise. When he was ten, Conor had served as model for the illustrations of an acquaintance, Jeanne Johns, for a children's book, *A Spy at Ti-conderoga*, by Clavin Fisher. Somehow our copy had been lost and, it being out of print but having been published by the Berkshire Traveller Press in Stockbridge, I had asked her to try to find a copy for us. Her search had turned out to be quite an adventure. She ran a classified ad in the local Shoppers' Guide urgently asking for help in finding a copy for Christmas and to her surprise had three responses by phone. When she told the callers the story of why she needed the book, they all insisted on bringing their copy by her bakery in Lenox. The deliveries, in the Christmas atmosphere of the small aroma-filled bakery, became quite emotional and all felt that they were privileged to take part in a real Christmas story, refusing to accept payment for these treasures. Then she went to the office of the publisher and there the staff burrowed through their archives and found the original proofs that had been used to make the book and presented her with those also. We went through the pictures with both tears and laughter—many of them were fine likenesses and they brought Conor freshly into our midst as more family arrived and looked at them.

In the afternoon we all went to the Pueblo again, for the Deer Dance, and then everyone arrived at our house bearing dishes for a grand Christmas feast. The guests even included eighty-five-year-old Greatgrandmother Lesley Brown—still, however, called Grammy by everyone, as she had always been by her literal grandchildren and my children as well, for whom she served that function when they were growing up. It is hard to imagine how we would have gotten through that and all of the following holidays without all of this family that we live in the midst of. And on this visit Kimry began to think of returning to Taos; it still felt like home to her.

David's solar design for our house proved to be eminently successful through its first winter test. We used only half a cord of firewood for social evenings around the fireplace and fires in the woodstove on the coldest mornings and have yet to turn on our official heating system of radiant heating beneath the floor tiles, though for much of the winter the temperatures dip below zero at night. The plants thrived in the greenhouse, the papaya tree produced fruit, and all the grandchildren have learned to swim.

In May the rest of the children paid us a visit. Amy picked up Barbara and her sons, Sam and Rafa, in Detroit and they all arrived for a busy two weeks of getting reacquainted with cousins and with new family homes, fishing in the Rio Grande, hunting staurolites in the Picuris Mountains, and other New Mexico adventures—the days filled to the brim, with much that had to be left for future visits when they finally piled into Amy's truck for the trip east again.

I had really forgotten the delight of spring in Taos; perhaps more than other seasons it is similar to spring everywhere. It was the spare and serene days of fall and winter that I had looked forward to as a refuge at the end of the long trek west—longer in years than miles, it seemed. I had almost forgotten about spring until it began arriving, bit by bit, between cold spells with frosty nights and even one episode of hailstones that turned the ground white for a while.

The snow patterns on the mountains receded again and again. Each time the air chilled and clouds covered the higher altitudes we thought that surely *this* would be the last snow. The warm spells were longer, but still the nights were cold and often the days also. When one of the late brief snows that showed only sketchily in the high valleys melted, the new lighter green of the aspen up there seemed to follow precisely the pattern of the snow that had lain there the day before; a last watering of snowmelt seemed to have produced that green. Finally the balance slipped to spring, though, and a mild day seemed a chilly spring one rather than a warm winter one, until finally it was no longer surprising to sit comfortably outdoors.

And I had forgotten the appearance of leafing green along the rivers and streams of the valley, the veins of green brightening every day, then finally creeping up the mountain slopes as the warm days passed, tracing the streams of the mountain canyons and finally the aspen pastures on the upper slopes. As the green deepened, the valley relaxed. There were days still when the wind blew from dawn until evening and it seemed utter foolishness to set out tiny plants or to water anything; then a short rain would freshen it all and days of calm sun would return.

The first blooms that we saw outdoors were in Conor's Garden—tiny crocus at the tips of the C. Then one day three bright yellow daffodils opened and were soon followed by several dozen more—so wonderfully sunny; then narcissus and white daffodils with crisp orange centers and purple and scarlet tulips filled the spaces in between. One morning we woke to an altered light that signified snow on the ground and looked out fearfully to check the blossoms. Each one was decorated with little tufts of snow precisely following the shapes of its petals, looking like yellow *and* white flowers. They looked perfectly happy though slightly ridiculous standing in the morning sun with a trimming of snow. David sprayed them with the hose to forestall frostbite, and after that the blooming continued uninterruptedly. We have a lot of work to do on that garden so that blooms will continue through the summer. My old friend, the photographer and writer Mildred Tolbert, invited us over to dig up some small trees that were crowding her orchard and we brought back, along with plums and some sizable apple trees, a half-dozen white lilacs that we set in at the back of Conor's Garden, to be a sort of backdrop and enclosure. Each bush came with a clump of flowers at its base, nameless now but recommended by Millie. On Memorial Day

Kristina came over before we were up and put in wildflower seeds all around the outer edge of the bed, then another day brought over blooming clumps of airy blue flax which we set in there also.

We rototilled and enriched the adobe soil in the flower beds beside the house with horse manure and straw from a farm down the road and with manure from Kristina's llamas. Then we moved all of our precious flowers brought from back East into those beds, to what we hoped was their final residing place. We left the comfrey, rhubarb, and horseradish at one end of the vegetable bed, set in some Jerusalem artichokes from Bob Grant's Dixon garden alongside them, and then David rototilled and refreshed the rest of the plot for this spring's planting. The dirt is now loose and springy, and it reminds me of the large vegetable garden of our neighbor, Mr. Morrison, back in Massachusetts. Our first spring there we had stopped to admire it—a rectangle of purplish-brown, perfectly raked soft-looking earth set in the midst of an already green meadow-yard. He picked up a handful of his garden and held it out so we could watch as it tumbled lightly from his hand, saying, "I made this." Watching the progress of his garden through the spring and summer was a ritual not only for us, we discovered, but for gardeners in that whole end of West Stockbridge. It was not at all our kind of garden, as we delighted in tucking things into odd places here and there and changing them around from year to year, but we were fascinated and watched neat row after row come up and go through its cycle in perfect order; it was the very essence of garden and the sight of a handful of friable soil will always bring to mind the picture of Mr. Morrison on his knees, arranging his earth around new spring plants; there was something god-like about it.

So the Spring Symphony of Conor's Garden has given us lovely music, ending with a healthy cluster of ranunculus near the path coming out with one more bloom each day in rosy red. Now we wait for irises and lilies and portulaca to come along, and for the bluebonnet seeds that we set in little patches to sprout. Those will be the first that I have seen for many, many years— in fact the last I *remember* were those that my brothers, Bruce and Miller, and I gathered great armfuls of in the open pastures of our childhood. Their color, the purest, simplest, blue—the most usual color of the sky, I suppose—has always been to me almost an *element,* not just one of the various colors, but a phenomenon in itself, and so engrained in my aesthetic coding that I don't actually recall *bluebonnets,* but simply receive directly the pleasure of that pure color.

The ditch in front of Jenny's house runs often, shallow in the bottom of its channel. Things that had for years been trimmed by grazing cattle throughout the summer when it was uninhabited land are now beginning to grow taller all along its banks. They must have wonderful root systems by now, having been pruned so often. Willow and wild rose are springing up along the ditch-bank and yellow lupin-like flowers that we'll transplant some of when they're through blooming.

I think often of individual spots and plants in our old garden—all the parts of it that we couldn't bring with us come to mind—but this gathering of new plants is also exciting. Every few days something appears; either we dig it up somewhere and bring it home for our wild garden or someone visits and brings along some roots or bulbs or thinnings. So the spaces are filling up gradually. Our dear friend Mary Alexander who, before her recent retirement spent many productive years as the director of the Taos County Welfare Department, has brought us great clumps of iris and, best of all, pure scarlet poppies, which David loves.

As our old flowers come to their full summer growth here, they are still slightly miniaturized even in their second year. This seems only wise; they are so exposed to sun and drying wind. These flowers and plants have moved almost as much as I have. Some of them—the peonies, the comfrey, and the euonymus—have been with us since the first home that we shared, moving as they grew, just as I did when a child.

There was one casualty in the moving, though. Some years back, Kristina and I took a trip to Scotland and as we drove south, finally, to York for the final rush by train to the airport in London, we went out to Holy Island on the east coast. There, while exploring the exterior of Lindisfarne Castle, which rose from the shore rocks on a sort of pyramidal hill, we spied, a little inland in the midst of a grassy meadow, a stone-walled rectangle that appeared to be a garden. It was, indeed, a lovely one with symmetrically arranged but rough-textured stone paving and plants in their late autumn colors sitting in broad beds of rich brown soil; and around it all was a high wall of rough masonry in the

TOP: *Rachel's first Weaving Southwest gallery. Tapestry with figures was woven by Kristina.*
BOTTOM: *The new Weaving Southwest gallery, north of the Taos Plaza.*

*The Rio Grande Weaving Supply section of the gallery, with
Rachel's hand-dyed wools on the shelves.*

lovely shades of English fieldstone, from palest tan and gray to rich russet. It must have been beautiful with full summer bloom against those stone walls, which protected the garden from winds off the ocean and from the foraging of the flock of sheep that dotted the meadow. The elderly gardener was a spry, quiet fellow, but he warmed to our questions and as we followed him around learning names and habits of plants he began snipping off bits and twigs here and there, then dug up a few things, and when we left I had a small plastic bag of treasures for my garden on Pixley Hill, seeds of wallflower and cuttings and roots of cotoneaster and Scotch broom.

The climate of Massachusetts is not too dissimilar to that of Holy Island and the plants grew large in a few years; then we sent a spray of broom home with Rochelle when she visited us and Jenny got it well established by her house. The casualty was the fine cotoneaster bush, which traveled too long in the sun and did not survive. I later learned, from a biography of the English gardener, Gertrude Jekyl, that she had herself created this garden in this exposed spot as a challenge and experiment. It seems fitting that some of the descendants of her plants are now in another exposed spot and at least one of them—the broom—seems to be extremely happy here.

Earlier, there was much talk of the low moisture accumulation in the mountains last winter, and the low water-level in the Rio Grande as compared with other springs; we decided to use part of the space in our new flower beds for vegetables and hold off on starting some perennials that we'd like eventually to have. So we'll be able to see the peppers turn red and the eggplants grow fat amongst the flowers and will have one tomato plant and a row of lettuce handy by the kitchen door.

My loom stands in the studio, but I'm still not ready for it. Rachel and Kristina, though are being very productive. Kristina has for several years now been weaving her new kind of tapestries—simple, bright figures of people and other creatures—delightful and dramatic. Their first impact is playfulness; then as you look, it seems that a more serious message is being communicated by the antics and juxtapositions of the simple, bright figures. They seem to be making some sort of down-to-earth philosophical statements, or perhaps just asking questions. She has always been fascinated with the forms of folk art, their simplicity and directness, and it seems that this quality of direct emotional communication is what she is after in her work, bypassing the complications of intellectualism. Often her creatures appear to be both human and animal, both male and female, hinting at the complexities involved in simply being human.

In between these tapestries she weaves rugs—still, she says, her favorite form of weaving. We decided to buy one of these for our living room; then she proposed that we do a trade, her rug for a sweater that I would spin and knit for her of her llamas' wool. So we took home the rug, and in between other things over many months I gradually transformed the wool from her llamas' coats into a warm ginger-brown sweater for their mistress.

Rachel has continued and developed the diagonals theme in her tapestries—varying in widths and intertwinings, in the wonderful colors that she dyes for her shop. But her main, more than full-time, absorption has been the development of her weaving-supply shop and her tapestry gallery.

In July she moved again. An ideal space farther north on the main street through Taos became available, and she decided to take the plunge. For several years she has had two devoted assistants, Ann Huston and Carol Greenspan, and recently another, Roxanne Blunck, and together they packed up and with Kinlock, Keith, David, and their three trucks transferred everything to the new space. Rachel, an apparently quiet, relaxed person, has the mysterious ability to take on mammoth projects and carry them out, step by step, according to plan and with loving attention to detail. Then by some appointed date all is accomplished, looking as though the achieved effect had been no problem at all.

When we all gathered for the big opening, the gallery—Weaving Southwest—was beautifully hung with tapestries; a large storage unit had been created which held more pieces to be rolled out for viewing, and around the edges of the room were rich stacks of woolen rugs and rows of colored pillows—the whole, spacious and utterly intriguing. Behind a partial wall resided Rio Grande Weavers' Supply. There the walls were lined with bins and shelves full of colored and natural yarns and spread over the rest of the room were her Rio Grande Looms with weaving in progress on them, other weaving equipment, large baskets of carded wool for spinning, and a corner for weaving publications, including *The Weaving, Spinning, and Dyeing Book,* her beautiful weaving manual, now in its third printing. We were *most* proud of her.

A few years ago, Rachel occasionally house-sat for a friend who had a computer, and she spent her time there learning to operate it, with some brief professional instruction. She loved it and what it could do and began working on a teaching manual for the group of craftwomen over in Los Ojos for whom she had supervised the creating of the Tierra Wools cooperative. The manual would be a detailed guide for learning all of the facets of the enterprise from setting up looms to designing, weaving, spinning and dyeing, and also bookkeeping and marketing, another typically monumental project. Now, of course, she has her own computer and uses it for her own business for bookkeeping and to produce her catalog, newsletters, and instruction booklets. And when her granddaughter, Teresa, sleeps over, she works with her own computer disk and is becoming very adept at it. It appeared to me at first a thoroughly martian contrivance, but she and others finally convinced me that it was simply an extremely useful machine and I now can't imagine writing without it, though I still, and probably always will, use only the base line of its talents.

Lorelei has done some weaving, too. She borrowed a loom from her mother and, with her, dyed up batches of yarn in light and middle sage greens and shades of chokecherry to weave a runner rug for their stairway, then also wove cloth for pillows and sofa covers. Their house has become a cozy combination of things New England and southwestern.

One of the pleasing family patterns that has evolved for us is Sunday family suppers at our house, when our children and grandchildren and Rachel come and share the preparation of the meal and catch up on what all of these busy people have been doing. And now we have a new child in the family. Rochelle's older half-brother, Todd, married a Taos Pueblo girl, Marlene Martinez, and they now have a small daughter, Lindsay Ann. Rochelle thoroughly enjoys being an aunt and we have become sort of honorary grandparents to this delightful small person. Periodically, especially for family birthdays, we have an Extended Family Supper and the group grows to include them, Kristina and her family, Seth and Kinlock, and often Malcolm as well. Now that Rachel's house is completed, some of these gatherings happen there or at

Kristina's. Having grown up far from any but immediate family, this is a happy custom for me, and quite the easiest form of entertaining. Our house has proven a perfect setting for groups of any size, with the children taking over some space to work or play at what intrigues them. Then when fall comes around, plans begin to form for where the holiday events will take place—this year it will be Thanksgiving at Keith and Lorelei's and Christmas dinner at Kristina's.

October 11

On Conor's birthday David and Kristina and I packed a lunch and, in Kristina's new 4-wheel-drive pickup, crossed the Gorge Bridge and headed toward Tres Orejas to spend the day collecting good rocks with which to border his garden—and just spend the day. It is beautiful, simple country; the land rises and falls gently, mostly sagebrush until you start to climb the rise to the mountain where the pinon begins. We stopped and wandered wherever it looked inviting and picked up craggy stones covered with gray and gold lichen—surprising out there in the exposed prairie—and collected quite an assortment of them. I have always loved that sagebrush land; for me it was a serene feeling to be dwarfed by the immensity of the space, the land and sky. I remember once returning to the west after living in the east for a while and realizing with surprise that here one *stepped on the sky* when one walked, that it came right down to the earth, whereas in the east it seemed to be up above somewhere and near the earth seemed air, but not quite sky.

Looking out in all directions we could see places where we had been on expeditions with Conor over the years. On a low, single-peaked mountain nearby we climbed once through the pinon woods, collecting pinon nuts. Further to the north was the grand, wide dome of San Antonio Mountain where David, Keith, and Conor once went looking for elk through the snow. Conor had gone alone to explore a canyon and spotted a group of elk coming downhill directly toward him. He leapt into a snowbank and burrowed into the snow so that only his head and shoulders were exposed behind a low bank of the arroyo and waited for them. They passed close by without noticing him and as the last elk went by he reached out and touched its flank—and it shot away.

Skirting the rise of the foothills of Tres Orejas, we discovered a valley behind it that we had heard and read of and saw a ranch "outfit" spread along its far side and a flock of sheep and scattered horses in the valley. The sheep, as we passed, left their pasture by walking under the sketchy fence, and soon we saw a horse and rider and two black and white sheepdogs tearing out from the ranch buildings toward them. We stopped to watch, and the voice that we distantly heard screaming curses and instructions to the sheep and dogs had a slight female sound to it. We parked and walked back, hoping to meet this wild cow-person. The dogs herded the sheep back under the fence, and she ambled her horse down toward us where we stood by the gate. Though noncommittal and a bit forbidding at first, she became quite friendly and, easing herself into a resting position in the saddle, talked with us for quite a while. Her mount was not a horse after all, but a fine looking reddish mule. Kristina later told us that people get very attached to a mule as a riding animal.

She told us the story of the valley and her family in it. Her grandfather had come into the area from Texas sixty years ago, when her father was six years old. He had worked on the excavation to create a lake in this depression that was fed through a small canyon that zigzagged in from the north, a government project in the twenties to make a lake that would hold the water and turn the surrounding area into farmland, primarily for growing beans. It was a grand broad lake until suddenly the entire body of water drained away into a sinkhole—and with it the fortunes of the farmers who had sunk their savings into the surrounding land.

The shape of the lake is still molded in the valley and the small canyon still feeds it, making in the spring a lake that lasts just long enough to irrigate well the land of the basin, then seeps away, leaving only a couple of small ponds along the course of the stream, the Rio Petaca. This irrigation provides for good fields of alfalfa through the summer and grazing for the horses, the flock of goats we saw, and the sheep.

The woman, probably in her late twenties, blond and rugged in jeans and boots, with her hair tucked up into a billed cap, over the course of half an hour told us quite a lot about her life out there. About eight years ago she and her father bought the ranch, the valley and land extending up for a way into the sagebrush, and they live there apparently very contentedly. Her brother owns the adjoining ranch and also runs an automotive repair shop outside of Taos. David realized later that Keith had talked of him, another rugged and dramatic character who told him wild stories of his younger days riding in the rodeo circuit. A mother was never mentioned in the conversation; the ranch was definitely her father's and hers.

The ranch buildings lay along the far side of the valley, a casual assortment of small buildings, a trailer, corrals, and a barn, its roof stacked high with hay, old vehicles settling into the land here and there. She told us that the sheep and the flock of goats were hers; the twenty or so sheep were orphan lambs that she hand-fed with goats' milk daily, two at a time. She said that her father would never use the ones that she had raised for meat.

Her saddle creaked as she shifted her weight and brought to me the memory of the smell and feel of saddle and horse hair in the sun and dust and space—a combination that I hadn't encountered in such a setting for many, many years, but which came back effortlessly intact.

We stood on the dirt road just outside the fence corner where she sat and at one point she got off her horse to inspect with us a land marker there. It wasn't until then that I noticed that she wore a gun. It was a small unornamented one, tucked in a simple holster, and I had the impression that she probably put it on right after her boots every morning. I asked her, "What do you use the gun for—rattlers and coyotes?" and she answered, "Yep, anything that moves and bothers sheep," which seemed potentially to include more than rattlers and coyotes. I was curious about the rattler population as I knew that this was the right kind of landscape for them and wondered when they went underground for the winter. Unfortunately, she assured us that they often found them out on sunny days even into the winter. "Killed one right up there behind you last week," she vividly added.

When David's daughters, Amy and Barb, and Barb's two sons visited us in the spring, Kristina invited us up to her cabin on this same foothill, a little farther south, and we had walked up the hill above the cabin. Winding our way amongst the sagebrush, I stepped on a softish clear sandy area and discovered, in a little hole, curious ropey things that I soon realized were baby snakes—

specifically rattlers, with one of the rattles visible. We had gone
on up the hill and on the way down I spotted some potsherds;
we discovered more scattered over an area of ten or so feet and
brought the collection home. We had been able to fit some of
them together and have planned to return to the site, hoping to
be able to find most of a pot and glue it into shape. I hoped that
this woman would tell me that it would soon be quite safe to
wander around that den with Rochelle, but evidently we'd best
be extremely wary or wear high boots.

We were fascinated with the conversation and talked on and
on, she seeming in no hurry. When finally we thought we should
move on, Kristina asked her if we might drop in if we were in
the area again. She didn't answer for a bit and then, as though
she had finally come up with a satisfactory answer, said, "Well,
I guess so . . . but we're usually working all the time." It was
said in a friendly way, but wasn't exactly an invitation. So we
said goodbye and strolled back to our truck as she took off at a
run across the valley.

We continued to explore around the back of the mountain,
entering Carson Forest through a wire-fence gate; we sat on a
rise to eat our lunch looking back over the valley, which now
seemed quite a romantic world to us. Behind us rose the highest
of the three peaks of the mountain and we decided to walk up it
a way since we were there. There wasn't really a stopping place,
so we ended up at the top, scaling laboriously the huge blocks
of stone that capped the peak. I didn't enjoy the last scaling—in
fact, found it quite hair-raising, but made it up; and from our
seats on large pieces of volcano-blown-apart rock we could see
far, far in every direction. To the east we could distinguish the
little settlement in which we live, see Taos and its sister villages
to the south, our Sangre de Cristos stretching on up to the north
and the first of the Colorado mountains, and the Rio Grande
Gorge nearby below us, jagging its way south below the mountains that stretch toward Santa Fe. Turning around, the cliffs of
the Comanche Rim were visible where they take a jog from their
usual facing to the west and then the valleys and mountains beyond.

My leg-brakes almost gave out on the way down, but I made
it and even managed to carry with me a few smallish volcanic

stones. As we bounced back on the rough road toward the bridge, Kristina said, "Conor would approve of the way we spent his day." Too tired to cook, we stopped for enchiladas on the way home. When we got there we found by the door a packet of tulip bulbs that Rachel had brought for Conor's Garden.

Celbia and Felipe

In midsummer Kristina's weaving studio and the yard that surrounded it were the setting for a five-day weaving workshop, which I eagerly attended. Celbia and Felipe, a young Peruvian couple, came from the small island of Taquile near the western shore of Lake Titicaca (part of the predominantly Aymara culture of this southeastern section of Peru, which for 3,000 years has been an important center of textile production) and conducted the workshop as part of a longer tour in this country. It was fascinating to me in many ways, even aside from the introduction to unfamiliar textile techniques. It was the first time that I had been in such a situation—had experienced such people—and it was the first time that Celbia and Felipe had left their country.

The purpose of the workshop was, of course, to learn something of what they knew—their textile skills. These skills are of a very high order, technically and aesthetically. In fact, in their work *technique* or *skill* has been brought to such a high level that it appears to be indistinguishable from *aesthetics*. Aesthetics seems not to be a consideration with them, not an aim but merely a natural result of the pursuit of their work, which apparently is the main focus and expression of their lives. The quality of beauty or aesthetics in this traditional work, developed in the distant past, has been blended with and carried by *skill* down through the generations; this excellence has been preserved as a cultural focus.

It seems that Celbia and Felipe and everyone else living on their island share an identity as textile craftpeople; that is, rather, their *present* identity. Before they were "discovered," working with yarn was less an identity than a fact of life. As a people, their skill with textiles has brought them respect. Now after ten or so years of contact with the world beyond the island—attention from the world beyond the island—they seem to be extremely conscious of this identity as very skilled craftpeople. I was curious to learn about their relationship to their work and its place in their lives, as well as learning something about the techniques of doing the work itself. One thing that was very apparent was that they were very proud of their work and very confident in their abilities; certainly there was no feigned modesty. I suppose that we, the students, made a special effort to show our admiration and respect for what they did. It was soon apparent, though, that their confidence was well-bedded in a sense of doing very well things that were the standard for accomplishment within their culture. They were good and they knew it—and they knew that the outside world knew it too.

There was a varying number of students attending the workshop each day—from six to ten. On the first day we met Celbia and Felipe as well as each other and Perla, our student-interpreter. Small frame looms had been constructed for us to use, adaptations of the type used on Taquile, which instead of being portable frames were horizontal beams held apart in tension by small posts driven into the ground wherever the weaving was going to be done.

Felipe was very friendly and cooperative and through Perla gave a little introductory talk about their life on Taquile. Celbia, who we thought didn't speak Spanish (she and Felipe conversed together in their own language, Quechua), sat quietly during this. We later learned that, just the day before, she had had several wisdom teeth pulled and did not feel at all well.

As there were a number of people warping up looms, I first joined the group who were learning to spin on the drop spindle with Felipe, stopping every now and then to watch the warping process which was more or less familiar to me.

The spinning was fun—it was very pleasant to spin yarn as one sat or moved around and wasn't too difficult to learn as I already knew how to spin on a wheel. All through the workshop I was to be *reminded* of the acute pleasure of really focusing on some process of working with materials, of being in rapport with them. I always enjoy spinning on my wheel, but found that this kind of spinning seemed really *more like spinning*—because, I suppose, it was the simplest, most direct, form of that activity. The simple light wood spindle and the wool and me, the purest form of the experience of spinning, the most direct enjoyment of the color and feel of the wool and the magical turning of the fibers into yarn.

Beyond the drop spindle each "improvement" in tools for spinning speeds up the process a little bit and to that extent dilutes the experience itself. On Taquile Island the spinners increased the speed of making yarn by developing skill, but they kept their spinning in their hands, which flew like birds in a great but silent hurry. Felipe dramatically showed us how fast and fine he could spin, then slowed down to show us how to begin, how to give the stem of the spindle a sharp twist so that its twirling could start the soft fluff of wool spinning.

On Taquile the men do much of the spinning, do the very intricately patterned knitting of hats and the weaving of plain cloth, called *bayeta,* for garments. The women also spin and they do the finer weaving—of belts and other patterned bands—all exquisitely woven of very, very fine yarn in traditional colors and designs, in patterns which were symbols for factors and events in their lives.

We were never able to determine exactly what was going on between us and Celbia in our student-teacher relationship. By the second day she was feeling better and we learned that she did understand and speak some Spanish. I started weaving on one of the belt looms, trying to master the complex sequences involved in creating the patterns. There was a comfortable feeling to the workshop; a jolly, affectionate rapport developed right away and Perla was a good bridge for us and for them. The atmosphere of Kristina's place contributed too—her weaving room, the yard outside where we also worked and the background of her llama farm, with mothers and babies peering over the fence now and then from the adjoining pasture.

Celbia's teaching was an interesting puzzle. As she began to feel better it became harder to tell how she really felt about this workshop. She did not seem to really be a teacher, in our terms. On the other hand, she *did* teach us—and I think that she gave us the experience of learning as the beginners did on Taquile. However, those beginners, who of course were children, learned by a gradual process of imitation and absorption over a period of years and we were learning in four or five days.

Learning the background-weaving technique was relatively

simple but the pattern which ran down the center of the band
was quite another matter. Celbia insisted that we learn it by the
method she was used to teaching—by watching her motions and
doing what she did. She vigorously resisted our attempts to figure
out a pattern or code to her movements, and especially opposed
our impulse to write down the sequence of thread-liftings that
produced the pattern. She seemed to be playing a guessing game
with us: when we were able to detect and repeat her system, we
would finally win the game. What worried us was that it seemed
quite possible that in the time we had we might very well *almost*
learn a very interesting technique.

At the same time she seemed a little perverse as she demonstrated with flying fingers how to select and pick up a set of
threads, so rapidly that we could not see exactly what she had
done, let alone commit it to memory. There had probably never
been a weaving student on Taquile who wasn't a child, nor had
she ever had to deal with an adult who hadn't learned in childhood. It even occurred to us that perhaps she really perceived this
teaching of private techniques to strangers as an invasion of privacy, and this even seemed reasonable. However, in spite of her
obscurity, we did begin to get a glimmer of insight into what
was going on. We finally learned that the fastest-fingered step,
which had so mystified us, was simply picking up *all* of the white
threads; and when we were finally able to proclaim, "Todo blanco!"
at the correct moment, she managed to acknowledge this unusual
spark of intelligence with one of her hesitantly lovely smiles.

I think that it enhanced the quality of the workshop that we
all had to court Celbia—that she was able to conduct her part of
it as she felt fitting, for whatever reasons. She was simply herself,
and spending time with her was a fascinating experience. We had
the privilege of being with her *as herself*, and instead of changing
her way of functioning she stayed put and let *us* relate to *her*. There
were no shortcuts, but it was a rich experience. She taught us
about the weaving developed by her ancestors on her island in
the way it was taught there, in the way she had learned it. We
learned from Felipe that Celbia had another teaching role on the
island; she conducted birth-control classes.

Felipe, on the other hand, was an eager teacher and was interested in relating to us. He was very proud of his island and its
accomplishments and was also involved in new developments

there. He was the head of the school board and was interested in some modernizations—for instance, to take back the means to charge their own batteries rather than traveling for three hours to the mainland coastal village of Puno to have it done.

Kristina helped Felipe set up a loom for weaving the bayeta cloth out in the yard, for which they made up some parts in her wood shop. He was fascinated with the power tools and, Kristina said, was very easy to work with, anticipating needs and moves as the construction proceeded. Then he and Perla prepared a warp, winding it around pegs driven into the ground in traditional fashion. Finally Felipe's loom stood warped in the yard and he began to weave bayeta and to instruct others on it.

Between her interpreting tasks Perla tried to learn the belt-weaving technique, trying to make notes that she could use later. On the last day she finally had time to warp a loom and begin weaving. When Celbia was not in the room, Perla told us of an encounter between them of which we had not been aware. Celbia had at first refused to help her and had finally told her why. Perla, particularly, had tried to put the construction sequence into written form, both as part of her translating job and in order to learn it herself so that she could make a belt later. Then when Celbia finally helped her on the last day, she told Perla that she had been angry at her for this, thinking that she wanted to write it down in order to take over her teaching role. So finally it came out that Celbia did value this role and did want to teach us.

When we were, on the second day, in the throes of trying over and over again to learn the proper sequence for the weaving steps to bring about the desired patterning with Celbia sitting among us, helping one and then another, Celbia said something to Felipe in Quechua as he passed by and he laughingly translated it to us through Perla. She wanted to tell us that when the children of Taquile were learning to weave and made a mistake she would give them a little slap to let them know that they must pay better attention. This became our joke, applying a rap to our hands when we knew we had made a mistake, and also our way of eliciting a smile from Celbia, letting her know that we were quite modestly conscious of our ineptitude. By the end of the last day everyone had some acceptable work to their credit and there was a subtle mellowing on Celbia's part; a few more smiles were exchanged. I will never be quite sure, though, whether they meant that she was a little pleased with us or whether she was a little pleased that to a degree she had kept her secrets.

I read later that it was the women of Taquile who were responsible for the perpetuation of the indigenous fabric tradition. It has been the men who have incorporated imported technologies, beginning with those from the Spanish—the treadle loom and the tailoring of garments, and now machine spun yarns and even synthetics. Looking back, these roles were very clear in our experience with Felipe and Celbia, and it makes me value even more, in retrospect, the experience of sharing to the degree that we did, Celbia's company and instruction.

Felipe told us that the men worked at farming in the mornings and did their textile work in the afternoons. During the time of the workshop his hands were constantly busy, either with knitting a hat or with spinning as he moved around. Both of these are time-consuming pursuits when this very fine yarn is used, so carrying them around to get a little work done as one walked made sense. It seems that fine, complex-patterned knitting appears all around the world where sheep are raised and need to be shepherded, and that yarn is usually spun while walking.

Felipe knitted his hats from the purl rather than the knit side, as we usually work with circular knitting, and it seems that it actually works more efficiently in the exchanging of pattern colors. As with all of their working systems, these Peruvians had invented very rapid and smoothly flowing ways of working. Felipe, working with two colors, passed them around his neck from opposite sides and tucked the yarn balls into his shirt pockets where the friction against his woolen garment kept just the right tension on the thread, and the knitting could hang safely to free his hands briefly for other things. He had begun knitting hats like this when he was a small boy and sped through the pattern changes without looking most of the time. In this, as in their spinning and other work, the efficiency of movement and the rhythm were fascinating to watch. Felipe was very intent on his work and seemed very content also; it seemed that he felt that what he was doing was important. As I watched him I imagined, behind him, his male ancestors back through time, moving through these same tasks, perfecting these techniques and these gestures, each impressing something of himself into the process and passing it on.

It is hard for us to imagine being part of such an ordered

system, being a link in such a consistent human chain—though there is a fascination in it too, something intriguing in imagining a life in which one moves from step to step in harmony with a patterned society. In contrast, it seems that we are each trying to *create* a society—to invent a philosophy, a religion, an occupation—to design a lifestyle to suit our "unique" personality and accommodate our individual goals.

We, as craftpeople, work with more or less unlimited choices of materials, of tools, of techniques. It seems that one of the most noticeable distinctions between a traditional society and one like ours is the number of choices to be made, and the experience of working with Felipe and Celbia was an intriguing glimpse of a kind of cultural peace. There is an elegance to their lives that they inherit: their beautiful and well-made everyday clothes, the graceful ritual of their days and their seasons, the luxury of a reality-based time scheme. Some variation of this picture is somewhere in our pasts, and when we meet it in the present, it is a potent experience. Here are the elements of our lives presented so simply that we can hardly recognize them, and yet what we see is also what we might come up with impulsively in trying to select the simplest, most important elements for a good life.

Now, when I imagine a South American marketplace—perhaps the one in Puno on the shore of the lake, to which the people of Taquile might go on market day—I imagine Celbia and Felipe there, maybe also with their two small daughters. I see them and others from their island spreading out belts and ponchos and knitted hats and their fine yarn. The market is full of such family or community groups, sitting on mats or blankets surrounded by their goods; perhaps there are foods, also, that they have brought to trade, some specialty of the island or simply a surplus.

What had never occurred to me before is that this marketplace is *full* of people who produce *museum-quality work* and have brought it here to show it and trade it and sell it with each other. We have craft shows that are designed to increase our reputations and/or make our living. Some, like marketplaces, are fairs held outdoors for selling and others are more formal exhibits, juried or by invitation. In Puno the work to be seen would identify the village or area where it was made; the work would *represent* the area. The craftperson would be competing with the standards set up by his village and through him the village would compete with others. Over the centuries there must have been myriads of subtle exchanges and influences passing from village to village by way of the craftpeople at these fairs—a slightly different twist applied to a drop spindle, some bit of a design that intrigued and even unconsciously became incorporated into the images of another village. The marketplace must be at least as important socially as practically, and it must have been historically crucial in creating a continuity of development and excellence in the textiles that amaze us today.

This workshop in itself was an interesting trade. "We" invited Felipe and Celbia here, more or less at Felipe's request, in order to learn about something that they knew and we didn't, because we respected their excellence. They wanted to come in order to learn something of solar energy-harnessing techniques and other means of solving power problems, as well as to gain financially by marketing work and establishing future possibilities for workshops. It is interesting to imagine that while here they may have gone into a shop in Taos devoted to the also very fine textiles of neighbors of theirs across Lake Titicaca to the south, in Bolivia. It would have been interesting to watch the two of them there checking things out and comparing them.

During the workshop someone brought in a handsome wide cotton belt woven somewhere in South America in a quite different technique from the Taquile weaving. Celbia and Felipe studied it for a few minutes and then dismissed it, showing no interest at all in this *aberrant* textile. We students, on the other hand, were fascinated with it. In fact, I realized that we seem to have an insatiable curiosity about different weaving techniques— which people all over the world knew, except for us. Perhaps it is partly our melting-pot mentality; we know that in there somewhere is *our* tradition, that we too have an intricate past, have rituals and group understandings; that embedded somewhere in our past is this knowledge of communicating with the world with our hands and eyes.

As I continued to muse over this experience, later, the element that most puzzled me was that of aesthetics—where its place was in the whole thing. It seemed such an integral part of the work and of the whole cultural presence that we encountered that I, at first, saw it as an intrinsic part of the whole process, almost a descriptive term for the most correct way in which a given task can be done. It seemed that tradition in craft work almost implied the presence of aesthetics. Then, finally, I realized that this quality of beauty had to be achieved at some point within a culture and then kept alive through tradition, had to be incorporated into traditional skills which could be passed down, becoming in a way then the *voice* of the culture, the way of preserving its highest achievements.

I don't know exactly how this corresponds to the function of aesthetics in other situations or places—ours, for instance. It seems a very different notion from the ones we function with. Is it that we make a separate subject of aesthetics, trying to (with the help of our "talent") insert it into our work at some point in its creation? Our work seems to be more in the nature of an exploration than what I have been talking about above. If it is that, then what are we exploring for, what are we in search of? Is aesthetics, then, some kind of magic keystone that tells us that our pursuit is a real one, a worthwhile one?

I think that it is not primarily cleverness, or practicality, or ingenuity that impresses us when we see skillful craft work from some specific and distinctive place. Our first reaction is "How beautiful!"—even before other reactions, such as "How clever!" or "How useful!" Somehow I think that it is some *combined* quality that we respond to. Perhaps it is some "evidence of integrity" in a made thing, which at every stage of its creation stamps it with an identity that we call aesthetic. This aesthetics is not an added or judgmental quality, but rather a recognition of a quality of aliveness, of integrity—of logic, even.

In making things we are in a way participating very directly with things outside our physical selves—other physical things than ourselves—a most basic kind of participation, a venture out into the world. This is one of the ways in which we blend with "that which is other than us"; I suppose it is relating. Here, "successful" would mean an interaction in which the intent of the person was communicated through the materials without destroying their intrinsic qualities—rather, highlighting them—or, put most primitively, paying tribute to them through noticing, which presumably is a noticing of a relatedness to them in the first place. It is a very complex area, obviously, and there are many variations involved in proceeding through the steps, say, from a primitive man making a whistle from a hollow stem to his carving and shaping and refining it. At first, only his breath goes through it, but later his impressions—some kind of additional communication—go into it.

It would seem that it is much easier to "see" or comprehend a part of oneself when it is a little separated—for instance, when we "put ourselves into our work." It is a useful pleasure to sit back after a piece of work is finished and, looking at it, try to comprehend what one has done. It is not pure flight of fancy to see most of our pursuits as attempts to make ourselves visible— to ourselves, basically. What is "Other than Us" is more visible, perhaps comprehensible, than we, ourselves, are—and in a way it makes sense that long, long ago man's *footprint* and then his *handprint* would arouse his curiosity as evidence of his reality, as a tangible form of his personality.

Art or Work?

Kristina, Rachel, and I participated in an exhibit at the Taos Art Association called *Textures,* an invitational show of weaving and ceramics. I dropped other work to weave my small tapestry, the first in four or five years, feeling that it was time to try being a weaver again and simply wanting to participate in the show. I bought two colors of Rachel's yarn that seemed a good beginning place to combine with leftover colors that I had on hand, so I wouldn't have to do any spinning or dyeing. It was fun to be weaving again, and the result was better than I expected, though not exciting—a presentable tapestry.

Rachel's weaving was a fine large horizontal tapestry from her series working with intertwining diagonals, woven with a group of the colors that she dyes for her shop, wonderful luminous middle colors. It was beautifully woven and serenely complex.

Kristina's three pieces were very good—one of her fanciful animal tapestries, bright in color, and another atypical one with a grid of white bands enclosing dark squares in each of which were clusters of bright colors. The third was a lovely rug, woven of heavy yarn she had spun—her first spinning, done in order to try to design the colors she would use right in the spinning by adding bits of carded color and variations of light and dark as she spun it—a continuous bulky strand of purples, ivories, and browns.

At the opening I wandered back and forth through the exhibit, trying to figure out my reaction to the work. A number of the pieces had some particular arresting quality; it seemed that the weaver was *after something* and this involvement was apparent and compelling. There were some pieces that were interesting in that the weaver was experimenting with construction possibilities, was really *working on something,* but simply had not yet brought all of the elements to a level where they communicated. And there were several fairly small pieces that I thought succeeded in the best sense of tapestry; they seemed to be straightforward communications through the medium of weaving.

My tapestry seemed to me, on seeing it in the show even more than seeing it on the wall at home, to be an *approximation.* There were a few places where it began to come alive, but the total seemed to be more or less aimless wandering, bits of thoughts that I had been through before but which were unrelated and out of context, not even a collection of good hints. The color, also, didn't really go anywhere. It began, but I never breathed life into it—probably because I decided not to take the time to spin and dye the *other* colors that became needed. Even with the colors I had, I probably could have made a good piece if I had become more involved. But I wanted to finish it, to get a tapestry made for this particular show and get back to the other work that I was really involved in. The result was thoroughly unexciting, and my accomplishment was that I learned not to do that again. One difference between the lack of success of my piece and what I felt was the partial success of some pieces in the show by more beginning weavers was that they were clearly working toward better integration of their intent and their experience; I had the experience to know better but didn't listen.

I guess that one of the things I learned or was reminded of in looking at the show was that, for me, working means that one has discovered a sympathetic or intriguing medium, that becomes a kind of voice one can use, with study and with *listening,* to unearth communications—to oneself first, and then perhaps to others—of what you are and are becoming and what and how the world that is your setting—the Other—appears to be. This is naturally a changing and evolving thing and the involvement in this process I think is the quality that can make a weaving or a pot or a painting compelling and *real.*

After the opening, we three and several other weavers had dinner in town, had a lively conversation on several subjects and a very pleasant time. The conversation jogged some rather sensitive points for me and I had to restrain myself from pursuing it too far, becoming too serious, and, instead, Kristina and I talked a little more on the way home. I think the point was that I was thinking theoretically, pursuing an idea, and the conversation was really about the practical concerns of weavers showing and selling their work in Rachel's gallery. The trigger point for me was the way in which the word "art" kept cropping up in the conversation. I realized that probably the difficulty was one of point of view; I had been working alone, trying to refine and distill ideas about working and they were talking about another facet of the weaving world—the specific practical concerns of presenting their weavings to the public.

One of their concerns was related to the long and continuing question of the status of their work, one that has a history of decades of controversy in the "craft movement." Craftpeople in various media have been struggling with the names given to what they are doing; specificaly, whether their work is "just craft" or whether they are to be called "artists" and their work to be considered on an artistic level with "fine" art, with paintings, sculpture, or music. The magazine *Craft Horizons,* in particular, has waged a war of terms and titles for craftpeople by using new nomenclature—for instance, calling weavers "fiber artists."

When Kristina, Rachel, and I began weaving tapestries— meaning, at least to me, weavings that were made specifically to be hung on the wall for looking at and having no function other than that and perhaps sound bafflement—there were two categories of weavings in the picture in this "art colony" of Taos: historic and contemporary. Historic weavings commanded a great deal of respect and were collected and prized both for their actual beauty and for their symbolic value as tangible evidence of the non-Anglo cultures in the midst of which we lived, which were an extremely important part of our reasons for living here. In fact, all craft work of quality that came from these cultural sources was highly respected—pottery, jewelry, ceremonial belts, among others. And because these objects of quality had been made in the past and the source for them was naturally limited, they were promoted from their original *useful* function to that of being *looked at.*

On the other hand, when referring to contemporary craft work the word "craft" underwent a complete reversal of meaning. It became a term of contrast to, loosely, the word "art" and was used to indicate a different and lower level of skill, seriousness, and importance. Onto this stage occupied by "art" and "crafts" we introduced another figure, "tapestries," which were in the simplest terms, woven pictures to be hung on the wall like paintings. Actually, there were three original figures on the stage, the third being indigenous crafts which even the "artists" gave the right to wall space. The problem, probably, was simply a historical one; a period of many centuries had passed since tapestries were made for hanging on walls. But now, for whatever reason, tapestries were again being woven and there was no automatic niche into which they fit.

Then, as the contemporary craft revival grew, a strange thing began to happen. Crafts produced that were intended to be looked at rather than used began to change in form. Whether this happened primarily to allow their makers greater artistic concentration and freedom or to separate themselves from the work of craftpeople who were still content to pursue their work as craft, I am not sure. But these workers who used materials other than the conventional "art materials" such as paints, canvas, paper, ink, stone, but who wanted nevertheless to be included in the category of "artists," began to alter the form that they gave their work. The best of them used their skill and involvement as well as ever and produced work with integrity, but many appeared to become focused on surface effect, on novelty, and to lose their relationship to their medium. They used the same materials but they tried to make them look like they were something else.

After mulling all of this over I realized that the problem really seemed to be not the branching out of those who worked in the "craft media" and produced "useful" things to making objects that were intended, rather, to be looked at and enjoyed as aesthetic or art objects. The problem was the coincidence of the popular craft revival with this transition that was taking place. Traditionally, craft standards have been somewhat strengthened by the innate necessities of the original reason for their creation—usefulness. It has always been a laborious process to make things—pottery or textiles, for instance—and they last longer and work better if they are made well. And the involvement of a skilled craftperson usually also results in the added quality of *beauty*.

Many craftpeople, even when labor-saving prepared materials became available (dyes and spun yarns, processed clay and glazes), continued to do all of this preparatory work themselves because it worked better or was more satisfying for them. But one of the unfortunate results of craft work becoming easier, coincidentally with the branching out from *useful* to *purely aesthetic,* seems to be that the popular following of the craft revival for some reason often has picked up on a surface interpretation of this transition to Art Crafts and bypassed completely the intrinsic standards of craft, which by dictionary definition means skill, ability, expertness; what is produced is a plethora of *things* that appear to be almost entirely surface gesture and ego-announcements.

A mystery to me in all of this is that it is such a big issue. Ming vases are considered works of art. Because they are beautiful. They convey—even explain—what fineness and excellence are all about. Fine Navajo rugs and other historic weavings are considered works of art. In a craft work that has survived the passage of time, physically and aesthetically, and because of its consequent value and rarity is now preserved as art object—there must be clues to this problem.

These craft objects are all useful as well as beautiful. Usefulness was originally part of their reason for being. So what gives these objects this other quality that is so important to us that we retire them from practical use and treasure them for it alone? An individual many centuries ago sat down at his wheel and turned a vase from clay, glazed and fired it. He was a potter. His lifetime ended and the vase survived. Hands from all of the generations that followed him have touched it, carried it, preserved it—because of something that went on in that short period of time in which he worked on it. Of course one of the things that went on was the use of skill that he had developed up to that time, perhaps a particular tradition of pottery making that extended for many generations behind him. But while he turned the pot, the skill resided in him. And he put it to use in combination with his individual idea and intent and feeling on that particular day—and made a good pot.

Perhaps he was competing with someone; perhaps this good pot earned him a job or a promotion; perhaps he made an even better one the next day or perhaps he never made another good one. None of this matters, really. His involvement employed his skill to produce a thing that has ever since represented something important enough to be preserved, even though it was only a pot—a craft object.

To some extent or other we all—we craftpeople or artists—

employ this kind of intent to communicate or record when we set to work. There are many things that can interfere with our success, either in the inner experience or the outward communication: distractions, practical problems, lack of skill, or simply temporary lack of focus or energy. But I think that the reason for being a craftperson or any kind of artist is the possibility of involving oneself in a tangible medium and then being able to look at the result that is produced and see some kind of record of that involvement, of that projection.

I have always had a problem with casual use of the word *Art*, with its use as a substitute for the word *Work*. At Black Mountain College, Albers told his students, "I can't teach you to be an artist; all I can do is help you learn to see." This was our pursuit—to learn to see and to give our visual study form in a medium. It was as simple as that. We didn't automatically become Artists when we began to use art materials, or even when we began to exhibit in galleries. We referred to what we produced as our Work, as our drawings or our weavings, our paintings or our pottery or our bookbinding. The question, "What do you do?" would be answered with, "I weave tapestries" or "I'm a painter" or "I'm a potter," assuming that the question meant "What kind of work do you do?" To answer "I'm an artist" would be not to answer the question at all, but to claim some kind of nebulous level of achievement. Art, or being an Artist, was not an identity, but a goal. It was a standard of integrity—a name, perhaps, for the direction in which we were heading, a sort of ultimate reference point with which to measure the steps we took in our work. So when someone says, "My art . . ." or "I'm an artist" I'm at a loss to know what is being said. I haven't learned what the person does, certainly not in any personal kind of way. All I have learned really is that they have a very casual relationship to the concept of art, but not what they are involved in.

The problem of making a living by one's work is a very real one. And being put into a lower category of importance that limits one's market—craftperson rather than artist—is naturally frustrating. But I think it is important to keep our terms straight in order to keep our standards and our integrity in our own control and thereby keep our goals intact. A poor painting is as poor as a poor pot. To claim to be an Artist in order to better one's market is a poor use of an idea which should, instead, be a source of private inspiration to go ahead with one's work.

Any worker in any medium has to deal with competition— from outside and, hopefully, from inside. All of the visual arts begin with craft. A painter goes to art school not to "learn art," but to learn the craft of painting. A composer must learn the craft of music; not every student of music becomes a great composer, but every great composer must have learned his craft in order to employ it to make great music. A stone sculptor's first job is to master the craft of working with stone. And throughout his career he will continue to struggle with the craft aspect of his medium, will work toward perfecting his use of his craft to produce something that will convey his intent, will communicate what is important to him.

A builder friend once said of a man on his construction job, "He's an artist with a bulldozer!" This statement has stayed in my mind because it seemed a totally acceptable use of the word artist in a surprising context. I usually don't refer to myself as an artist because rather than being a true comment on my accomplishment it would be a casualizing of my intent. In this remark, though, it really signified something. The man was skilled, probably loved his work and had a talent for it—and his involvement produced a glorious result. That, to me, is *being an artist*.

One of the most valuable parts of the experience of being at Black Mountain College for me was that of studying and working in an educational community where the emphasis was on working at something—anything—with devotion and curiosity. Those were the criteria of value, and in that atmosphere to differentiate between disciplines as to worth would have amounted to a kind of racism. We all, I suppose, hope to in some measure, at some point, achieve fineness in our work, but what is really exciting is the feeling that we are growing, that we are discovering things that we hadn't known before—and especially that there is so much ahead that has not been realized. And, for me, Art is the name of a direction, not a product. Perhaps the decision as to whether an individual piece of work—a painting, a pot, a sculpture, a weaving—is a work of art should be left to others, and to time.

Fortunately we are somewhat insulated from the marketplace by the people who direct galleries and showrooms and museums and their talent for creating an environment that helps to identify our work with standards that we find acceptable. Rachel's gallery—Weaving Southwest—is one of the places that has brought things in this one small town full circle from the days, some thirty years ago, when we three began to weave tapestries in a community that specialized in painting, drawing, sculpture, and other "art media" but had no niche for other than *historical* work in the media of "crafts." The craft revival in this country has been a veritable explosion, one that has also reverberated backward, reviving historical traditions. Spanish and Indian craftpeople are now part of the contemporary craft movement, some linking their work to historical tradition and some directly joining the contemporary mainstream. The quality of much of the work is at least as high as that of much of the "art work" in the valley. Standards are high and competition is keen and consequently the boundaries between media begin to disappear or become meaningless. It has been a period of amazing change and growth. Not only has there been stimulus from outside—with the Southwest becoming known for fine craft work—but also from within the area, where the number of craftpeople who find this a stimulating place to work and live provides its own impetus for exchange, exploration, and growth.

Present and Future

When I look back over our residence here, sometimes I can only realize that we have been in Des Montes for four years by recalling the Christmases—the first without Conor in our little two-room structure, the second when Kimry and John were here, the third after which Kimry came to spend a week with me while David went with Keith and Lorelei again to Baja for fishing, and the one just past, when we happily welcomed a new family member, John Seaver, Jenny's fiance, who lives in Santa Fe.

David's daughter, Barbara, and her sons, Sam and Rafael, spent most of last summer with us, and during that time grew to love it so that they decided to move to New Mexico. Now they live in the little house beside Keith and Lorelei's, and Barb has taken up jewelry-making. For Christmas they acquired two young burros, who now share Keith's barnyard with his three horses. Now Sam, as well as Rochelle and Teresa, goes to the nearby Arroyo Seco school. Amy is still a determined New Englander, but will soon arrive for a long post-holiday vacation from her bakery. Kimry and John think of returning but are not ready yet for the move.

David has almost finished building the little room that he, with Barb's help, added onto his shop last summer, which we call the Loom Room. As well as looms, it will contain a guest bed, and Amy will be its first inhabitant. She is bringing with her my second loom—a small one that Kimry has been storing for me. Weaving plans are piling up in my thoughts, and I begin to believe that I will actually get back to work with the coming of spring.

In December Kristina and David shared an exhibit at Clay and Fiber Gallery in Taos, a show of their very different kinds of work in wood. Kristina's pieces were the painted wood collages that have evolved from her fanciful woven allegorical tapestries. The last piece that she made for the show was called The Flores Family, a low-relief scene of the figures of a family standing on their portal, complete with shaped corbels above the posts, in which the father of the family wears a belt for which Lorelei fashioned a tiny silver concho buckle.

David's sculptures were mostly lathe-turned pieces in natural woods. In some of them he laminated seasoned wood into cores—especially interesting pieces collected on wood runs or brought with us from the East—and then on the lathe worked with the elaborations of natural patterns thus produced, a kind of geometry in motion with the shaping on the lathe. His largest piece was a room-divider-sized one of standing columns stenciled in patterns, contained within a framework so that they could be turned to produce seemingly endless configurations. This piece, called Changes, stood at the end of our greenhouse until time to assemble the show and when it was taken to the gallery, Rochelle said, "I hope it comes back; it looks boring in here." It was a beautiful exhibit of contrasting work, and after the opening we had supper and a party at our house to celebrate their accomplishment.

For me this has been a time of coming to terms with going into the future, with making plans for returning to weaving. Perhaps until now I have been unable to see a future without Conor; the loss of my son has seemed a negation of the future, has made the future appear to vanish. Now, as I come to the present in this story of what has happened in our lives over time—people loved and lived with, work enjoyed and developed—I find that I have simply been led into this present, and that it is the threshold of a future that already begins to construct itself; I must go ahead. And strangely, I have begun to feel that Conor is involved in this facing of new discoveries to be made—that he is urging me on, is saying "Go for it!"

When Kimry was here for a week with me last winter, we looked at a lot of Navajo weavings together, particularly the beautiful, simple, early ones. We tried to comprehend the ways in which these wonderful pieces accomplished such satisfying divisions of the woven surface—to grasp the subtle variations of diagonals employed, to follow the proportions of the bands and stripes that seemed so effortlessly correct. I came to feel that these rugs carried the feeling of a weaver in the midst of a large space, who, as she carried the yarn forward, was in some way traveling over the space in which she lived, unconsciously measuring and comprehending—*associating with*—this large world that was her home. And I decided that I wanted to explore in this way, to try to learn what I could from it.

Last spring David and I visited the Grand Canyon and seeing that incredible occurrence for the first time was a stirring experience for me. I realized that I had woven tapestries about some of the subtleties of its grandeur, though what I had then seen to suggest these kinds of forms were bits and pieces of related geological happenings here and there over more familiar areas of the Southwest, which here seemed to have been but the edges of a picture of time and space that now lay before me, all in one piece.

Then, on our way home, we passed through the broad, open, horizontal spaces of eastern Arizona and northwestern New Mexico—land of the Navajo—which appear less geologically eventful, and yet contain, in distilled form, all of the drama of that great gash, meted out, it seemed, bit by bit. The Grand Canyon seemed an epic geologic poem, containing all of the stories of millions of generations of events, including in its vastness the elements of time and of change still legibly written. But this simpler land seemed to me, then, the place where one could *live* with the evidence of these realities. Here, a whole section of land might be devoted to the accomplishing of a rise in the land of a few hundred feet; here, one could feel oneself as *within* the visible world, rather than a spectator. I think it was then that I began to wonder what one would weave when sitting outdoors at a loom in the midst of land with this lovely simplicity—what we sometimes call "emptiness."

So I will soon begin to set up my new weaving room, move the looms and my Rio Grande Wheel into their places, spread out my accumulation of yarns where I can see what they have to offer, and then put on fresh warps and begin to spin—the best way, for me, of beginning to *think weaving*. On the narrower warp of the small loom I'll begin to work at what Kimry and I optimistically call my "Navajo studies." They will be not rugs, but simply explorations, and I have no idea now of what they will lead to; I'll just be trying to learn something from the anonymous Navajo weavers whose work impresses me so.

My other weaving plans are of a much more practical nature—simple, sturdy wool cloth for blankets or bedspreads, beginning with just white and brown yarn and then perhaps dyeing up some colors. I've looked forward for a long time to doing such weaving, thinking of it luxuriously as weaving "heirlooms" for my children. And also I want to weave bright-colored rag rugs for our kitchen from my stockpile of old cotton jersey shirts, which Rochelle will help me cut spirally into weaving strands. David searched for weeks and finally found an old iron cookstove with which to heat the new room, a small yellow and green enameled one which looks cheerful and doesn't take up too much room. It will be a cozy place in which to begin to think and to work.

Rachel, Kristina, and I have sat down together for several evenings of talking about our work and our plans. At first we simply talked about the surprising experience of finding ourselves in our sixties. For Kristina this has been a puzzling experience, with conflicting feelings. She has more time than ever before and has been very physically active, hiking and skiing, and is deeply involved in her work with the wood pieces that have largely replaced her tapestry weaving. Now those have evolved into free-standing sculptures, and ideas come piling one upon another, faster than she can construct them. But she misses the work with people that has always been so important to her—inventing projects to get people involved in weaving—and the structuring of her life that this involved.

Rachel's life is definitely busy enough, and her work is gratifying and successful. If there is a lack, it is for time simply to contemplate and more leisure for doing things with her grandchildren. Nevertheless, she is about to begin a new project. A few months ago she offered to work with a drug-rehabilitation center in the Española Valley, called Delancey Street—first supervising the building of looms in their well-equipped woodworking shop, then helping them set up a weaving workshop and teaching them to weave. Now Kristina has volunteered to help her in this project, so her excess of unstructured time will soon be remedied.

Looking back over the forty-odd years since I first came to this beautiful valley and the more than thirty years that Kristina and Rachel and I have been working together here—more continuous for them than for me—I see a vast tapestry of events and people, of work begun and developed and changed, all woven into this landscape that we have loved and all connected for us by the woolen threads that we have worked with over these years.

Our lives have been intertwined through our work and our shared life patterns, and we each have been deeply affected by the rich cultural setting—Spanish and Indian—in which we have been privileged to live. We have adopted ways of weaving from these cultures and the integrity of their craft tradition has been important for us as we developed our own ways of working. One cultural aspect that has been particularly sympathetic for us is the integration of working and living, which we found still a pattern here, one of the reasons for our choosing this out-of-the-way place to live.

Though it was not a conscious intention when I began to write about the three of us as weavers, I find that the story has become more than that of three women's careers. Many characters have entered the story as it proceeded through time; children, then grandchildren, have given our lives dimension. We have encountered delight and we have encountered trama—all of us—and now all of the elements out of which these years have been created seem to be interdependent parts that together are our story—the story of three weavers.

Afterword

Looking back over the weaving of all these years, I see expanses of warps strung back in time—warps of linen and of wool and of cotton, wide ones and narrow ones—and I remember the excitement that each produced. Each was a web of strings that awaited the weaving of songs—like an instrument, tuned and ready—on which we could play out the delight of color and form and texture. With each new warp we strung, we planned a new adventure, a new exploration; each was a framework in which we would spend a period of time, in which we could somehow define the present and its intentions. These warps have been good companions, friendly borderlands where we could work, back and forth as in a garden, season by season as our lives grew over the years, each new present leading into the plans of an intriguing future.

Index